T0305762

Decoding
Economic Crises

DECODING
ECONOMIC CRISES

Cristina Peicuti
Jean-Marc Daniel

ESCP Business School, France

World Scientific

NEW JERSEY · LONDON · SINGAPORE · BEIJING · SHANGHAI · HONG KONG · TAIPEI · CHENNAI · TOKYO

Published by

World Scientific Publishing Europe Ltd.

57 Shelton Street, Covent Garden, London WC2H 9HE

Head office: 5 Toh Tuck Link, Singapore 596224

USA office: 27 Warren Street, Suite 401-402, Hackensack, NJ 07601

Library of Congress Cataloging-in-Publication Data
Names: Peicuti, Cristina, author. | Daniel, Jean-Marc, author.
Title: Decoding economic crises / Cristina Peicuti, ESCP Business School, France,
   Jean-Marc Daniel, ESCP Business School, France.
Description: Hackensack, NJ : World Scientific, [2024] |
   Includes bibliographical references and index.
Identifiers: LCCN 2023039693 | ISBN 9781800615106 (hardcover) |
   ISBN 9781800615113 (ebook for institutions) | ISBN 9781800615120 (ebook for individuals)
Subjects: LCSH: Financial crises. | Crises.
Classification: LCC HB3722 .P444 2024 | DDC 338.5/42--dc23/eng/20231005
LC record available at https://lccn.loc.gov/2023039693

British Library Cataloguing-in-Publication Data
A catalogue record for this book is available from the British Library.

First published 2024 (Hardcover)
Reprinted 2024 (in paperback edition)
ISBN 9781800615700 (pbk)

For any available supplementary material, please visit
https://www.worldscientific.com/worldscibooks/10.1142/Q0446#t=suppl

Translated from the French by Malcolm Leveridge
Desk Editors: Logeshwaran Arumugam/Ana Ovey/Shi Ying Koe

Typeset by Stallion Press
Email: enquiries@stallionpress.com

Printed in Singapore

"Who knows what the tide could bring?"

Tom Hanks in *Cast Away*

Translated with the support of
BPCE Chair "Mutual and Cooperative Banking
for the Benefit of the Economy" at the ESCP BS.

About the Authors

Cristina Peicuti foresaw the 2008 crisis, which was the subject of her thesis, "The subprime mortgage crisis and the credit channel" (Paris, Panthéon-Assas University, 2006–2009). An affiliate professor and a scientific director at the ESCP Business School (Paris), the oldest business school of France, she is an economist in a mutual and cooperative bank. In addition, she is the chair of the Strategy and Corporate Social Responsibility Committee of the Realités Real Estate Group and serves as an adviser to the French government on foreign trade. She is a member of Société d'Économie Politique, one of France's oldest learned societies, concerned with political economy. Cristina is the author of the books *Credit, Destabilisation and Crises, Decoding Economic Crises* (2024) and *Of Banks and Crises* (2024).

Jean-Marc Daniel is an emeritus associate professor at ESCP Business School. He serves as the president of the Société d'Économie Politique. He regularly offers his insights as a commentator on *BFM Business* and contributes as a columnist to *Les Echos*.

Contents

Introduction

> "The inherent vice of capitalism is the unequal sharing
> of blessings; the inherent virtue of socialism is the equal
> sharing of miseries."
>
> — Winston Churchill

Is the market economy stable by nature? What happens to make it unstable? Is it external shocks, such as pandemics or wars? Is it the incompetence of policymakers or regulators? Or is this instability inherent to the market economy's very dynamics and/or mechanisms? Does the market economy carry the forces and seeds of its destabilisation? If so, will this destabilisation prove fatal, as Marx and communist theoreticians believe? Is there an alternative to the market economy? Or do these upheavals merely require patience on the part of economic agents and policymakers, long enough for negative effects to be cushioned?

It is easy enough to criticise the market economy. Many thinkers have announced its demise, bemoaning or rejoicing at the prospect. However, since the mid-18th century, the Western world has experienced strong growth thanks to the market economy's existence in more or less modified forms. Growth has not prevented economic fluctuations and crises to this day.

At the end of the Second World War, through the Marshall Plan, the United States helped the western half of Europe recover and continue to develop based on a market economy. The other half of Europe, "liberated" by the Soviet Union (only to be brought under its yoke), did not have the opportunity to benefit from the Marshall Plan.

The United States administration gathered the negotiators of 17 European countries and oversaw the implementation of the Marshall Plan from 1948 to 1950 from the Hotel de Talleyrand, the Paris mansion located between rue Saint-Florentin and place de la Concorde, home of the great French statesman after whom it is named, where he entertained heads of state and international dignitaries and where he passed away.

Talleyrand pulled the strings at the Congress of Vienna after Napoleon's defeat and even during the Hundred Days, when he managed to convince the European victors not to leave the negotiating table, claiming that Napoleon would not remain in power for long! After the Second World War, it was the United States that pulled the strings, fittingly from the Hotel de Talleyrand, which served as headquarters for the Marshall Plan.[1]

After 1945, the USSR imposed a classical Soviet-type command economy on one half of Europe. Populations in Eastern Europe (or strictly, Central Europe, a hotchpotch of cultures, languages and economies), in opposition to Western Europe, were forced into a so-called communist economy, turning their backs on the market system.

By the time the Berlin Wall fell in 1989, the economic performances of former Soviet Bloc countries bore testimony to the aberrations of a planned economy. The communist era from 1948 to 1989 was a political, moral and economic tragedy for Eastern Europe. This tragedy is plain to see in the case of Czechoslovakia, a country with a rich industrial heritage and whose economic development before 1939 was comparable to that of

---

[1]At the time of the Marshall Plan, the Hotel de Talleyrand belonged to the Rothschild family. The United States acquired the mansion on 14 November 1950 to house its embassy and later the Marshall Center, home to a unique exhibit honouring the pivotal European contributions to the success of the European Recovery Program, better known as the Marshall Plan. More than 70 years later, the mansion is still home to the United States embassy. In the intervening years, the United States has ruled supreme, playing a central role in international diplomacy and the world economy. No matter the sheer scale of the Marshall Plan and communication efforts surrounding it or the United States leadership since then, the stately mansion remains named after the great French statesman, not the United States Secretary of State. Talleyrand's wish, "I want people to continue discussing for centuries what I was, what I thought, what I wanted", has thus been fulfilled, much to the chagrin of the United States, for George C. Marshall cannot lay claim to such as august a legacy.

Western countries. In 1948, when the Communist Party assumed undisputed control over the government following a *coup d'état*, per capita income in the country was higher than in Western Germany and 85% of per capita income in France. By the time of the so-called Velvet Revolution in 1989, per capita income in Czechoslovakia was 60% of per capita income in Germany and 62% of per capita income in France. After 1989, not one former "socialist country" continued to base its development on a command economy. All swung from one extreme to the other, from a command economy to a liberal economy.

One might say of the market economy what Winston Churchill said of democracy: "It has been said that democracy is the worst form of government except for all those other forms that have been tried from time to time".

The market economy that existed in Europe and the United States before the Second World War, which the latter imposed on the world in the post-war era, prevailed. Of course, historical circumstances mean that it has been fashioned on the lines desired by the United States. Post-war, this country has been the great artisan of globalisation.

Notwithstanding this success, large-scale crises reminiscent of the Crash of 1929 have rocked capitalist economies since 1945. The world economy experienced recessions (contractions in activity) in 1975, 1992–1993, 2009 and 2020. Public authorities proved incapable of preventing the crises (1929, 1974, 1991 and 2008) that had preceded these recessions. That being so, they had to heal what they could not prevent. One question is whether globalisation and what some have called the "financialisation" of the economy contributed to the propagation of these tremors in increasingly interlocked economies at the global level. These global crises have led to massive interventions by states — what might be called state interference — and central banks, which gradually affirmed their independence. The very fabric of the market economy has been distorted as a result. To function optimally and for economic agents to find meaning in their involvement, the market economy needs to remain labour- and competition-based. Instead, it is structured increasingly around the accumulation of debt, particularly public debt.

Having proved incapable of preventing the onset of crises, the question is whether governments and regulators have at least been able to contain these phenomena. In particular, have they drawn lessons from each crisis to better deal with the next one and mitigate toxic aftermaths? There was the debt deflation after the Great Depression, the stimulus plans in 1975 based on the locomotive theory developed by the OECD, Japan's recourse to quantitative easing in 1992–1993 before the wider adoption of this monetary policy during the 2008 crisis and the Pandemic Emergency Purchase Programme in 2020. Were these cures or just band-aid solutions? Were these responses rational or arbitrary? Ultimately, is capitalism such as we know it all about competition (and may the best win!)? Or is it a matter of connivance, with the state favouring one or other economic agent and kicking the problems down the road? Is the limitless recourse to debt underpinning the economic system an instance of what communist theoreticians call "state monopoly capitalism"?

Understanding the origins of crises, their evolution, their resolution and their necessity will, in turn, help comprehend today's world. One can adapt instead of nervously blundering blindfolded through a crisis. One can grasp not just the risks but also the opportunities and thus take advantage of a crisis.

Each crisis has its winners and losers. To identify the big winners and losers, one needs only to consider the breakdown of global wealth before and after the 2008 or 2019 crisis.

A subsidiary question is whether countries that have carried the day can hold on to their gains. Can anything be inferred about their capacity to lead the world economy? In the 19th century, Britain dominated the world economy, with its vision of the economy based on classical/neo-classical liberal theories. Since 1945, it has been dominated by the United States, based on a Keynesian justification for the systematic use of budget deficits and easy money. American economic leadership was not fundamentally challenged by the Soviet countermodel and its avatars. Will the pounding inflicted by the 1992, 2009 and 2020 recessions deal a blow to this leadership to the benefit of the authoritarian capitalism that has flourished in Asia? Or will environmental challenges usher in a more devastating crisis reminiscent of the "nutritional trap" theorised by Nobel Prize winner Angus Deaton? Will there be a return to times of absolute scarcity and famine prevalent before the mid-18th century?

Part I

Can the Economy Exist Without Crises?

"We cannot solve our problems
with the same thinking we used
when we created them."
— Albert Einstein

Chapter 1

There Have Been Crises Since the Dawn of Time

"There is nothing new under the sun", *Ecclesiastes* 1:9. Crises are no exception. They are a perpetual repetition, to the point that they fit into another phenomenon: market economy cycles. This repetitiousness begs the question of what the economy would be like without crises. Would the economy even exist? Would it present a degree of sustainability?

Modern crises are often financial crises. They generally start with a rise in the price of an asset that is limited in nature to a level that is increasingly above that asset's intrinsic value. The inflation in the price of the asset is fuelled by the fact that related purchases are often made on credit in the United States. During the crash of 1929 and again in 1992 and 2008, the asset in question was real estate. The spectacular rise in prices encouraged more and more economic agents to buy real estate in the hope of reselling it later at a substantial profit. The rise in prices is out of all proportion. As the German proverb goes, trees don't grow to the sky: the speculative bubble[1] ends up bursting, and the market goes into reverse. What follows is a sudden and dramatic plunge in the price of the asset, back towards its intrinsic value. It may even fall below this value because of an overabundant supply of this asset in the face of weak demand, with mistrust taking hold. As the American billionaire and

---

[1]The term "speculative bubble" dates back to the start of the 18th century. It was coined by the British authorities in reference to the speculation surrounding the stock of the South Sea Company and the subsequent collapse in the stock price, the episode becoming known as the South Sea Bubble.

businessman Warren Buffett put it, "only when the tide goes out do you discover who's been swimming naked". What is important is that what starts off as a financial correction leads to a crisis: the frailty of the economy at macro- and microeconomic levels is laid bare for all to see (at the global and country levels, as well as at the level of businesses and households). In fact, it is when the purchase of assets at exorbitant prices has been financed on credit that the crisis really begins because selling the assets is no longer enough to repay the credit. As a result, banks are also undermined. They find themselves quite unable to continue financing the economy, even though it is already in difficulty. This was the scenario in the crises of 1929, 1992 and 2008.

Such speculative bubbles have existed since time immemorial. There were already instances in ancient Rome. In AD 33, during the reign of Emperor Tiberius, Rome's financial system experienced a crisis, the first for which there are quite precise accounts of its unfolding. This was a credit crisis: creditors called in loans in order to purchase land (to meet a requirement under a lapsed but now revived decree that conditioned usury on part of the lender's capital being invested in land), which led to a large number of defaults as debtors could not raise the funds. Such was the scale of the crisis that the Roman State stepped in, meeting the debtors' obligations towards their creditors. Amounts owed by debtors now had to be repaid to the state. Also, the state injected liquidity into the system by channelling funds through specially chartered banks that offered three-year, interest-free loans. In this way, creditors avoided bankruptcy as they recovered from the Treasury what they were owed. Debtors also avoided bankruptcy: their debt subsisted but was now sustainable. To the extent an estimate can even be drawn up, these measures cost the equivalent of 0.5% of the Roman Empire's gross domestic product.

The first speculative bubble to have captured the public's imagination for generations was probably the Tulip Bulb Market Bubble in the 17th century. It occurred in the United Provinces (present-day Netherlands). The craze for tulip bulbs led to an irrational rise in their price, which reached a peak in February 1637. A word — *tulpenmanie* in Dutch, or "tulipomania" — was even coined to describe the frenzied buying that gripped the country between 1633 and 1637. During this period, the price of tulip bulbs increased fivefold between 12 and 25 November 1636. Then, it doubled again between 25 November and 3 February 1637, the day on which prices began to fall. On 3 February, the price of a tulip bulb represented 10 times the annual salary of a Dutch craftsman in those days. By 1 May 1637, the price had returned to its level of early November 1636. The first modern episode of generalised speculation, tulipomania, continues to feed the theoretical reflections of financial specialists to this day. This founding act of what is known as "speculative hysteria" was followed by other speculative bubbles, mainly due to the evolution of the public debt.

When, to the king's surprise, a speculative bubble burst at the start of the 18th century in France, the monarch asked Voltaire for an explanation, which he provided in one sentence: "paper money eventually returns to its intrinsic value, your Majesty".[2]

Financial crises are a very old problem. They are often presented as the alpha and omega of the crises that have shaken the economy. Though financial crises have captured the imagination, before the Industrial Revolution, the most devastating crises for the population were subsistence crises. The "nutritional trap" theorised by Angus Deaton refers back to this era. Extreme and general scarcity of food leads to dramatic rises in prices. The crisis, whether due to speculation or to an absolute scarcity linked to poor harvests, results in a sharp rise in the prices of certain commodities, leading to a considerable redistribution of income and plunging large swaths of the population into misery.

With the onset of the Industrial Revolution, the economic growth of industrialised countries was marked by crises that were not strictly financial, unlike those caused by food shortages. They started as "industrial" crises, characterised by a phase of overproduction, followed by a correction that resulted in a contraction of production. In the 19th century, the periodicity of these crises was, on average, decennial: 1816, 1825, 1836, 1847, 1857, 1866, 1873, 1882, 1890, 1900, 1907 and 1913. As early as the 1820s, this periodicity meant that the notion of crisis was fairly systematically associated with the idea of an economic cycle. One of the issues with which economic theory is still grappling to this day is the regularity of the slowdowns in growth, or, put another way, the relevance of the cycle concept. Are these repeated slowdowns wholly fortuitous or attributable to the very functioning of the market economy? This question shows that an understanding of crises requires an analysis of economic cycles.

In 1926, in his book entitled *The Major Economic Cycles*, Soviet economist Nikolai Kondratiev [1892–1938] postulated that there are long economic cycles, lasting between 50 and 60 years, which comprise

---

[2] Orieux, Jean (1999).

three phases: expansion, lasting 20–25 years, followed by a short turning point, and then depression, also lasting 20–25 years. This theory had the favours of French economist and sociologist François Joseph Charles Simiand [1873–1935], who considered that during a phase A, there is a rise in prices accompanied by sustained growth in production, and then, during a phase B, there is a fall in prices, followed by slower economic growth. These two phases follow each other. However, other contemporary economists, such as Wesley C. Mitchell,[3] considered them simply business cycles of varying duration. Paul Samuelson [1915–2009], the recipient of the 1970 Nobel Prize in Economic Sciences, dismissed the Kondratieff cycle as "science fiction".

After the First World War, econometrics was enlisted to try to quantify crises and cycles. The intention was to adopt as scientific an approach as possible in determining the relevance of the notion of cycle and identifying its periodicity. This meant developing statistical methods using quantitative data to predict economic fluctuations, cycles and their regularity. One of the presuppositions of the econometric approach is admitting that such predictions do not provide a theoretical, rational justification of cycle mechanisms but a simple empirical description.

Economic research thus became a major issue for economists and one of the aspects of their work most visible in the public debate. The creation of the National Bureau of Economic Research in the United States in 1920, the Institut fur Konjunkturforschung in Germany in 1925 and the Service d'Observation Économique in France in 1937 illustrate the development of this new branch of economic science. Academics were involved in this development. For example, in the 1920s, Harvard University developed a barometer of business conditions that was supposed to forecast the evolution of the economy. As disappointing as the results of economic forecasts proved, as they were often invalidated, econometrics became a major branch of economic science. It is now systematically used by economists to the point of being indispensable. At the same time, more and more institutions, such as credit rating agencies, are combining big data and artificial intelligence to forecast economic fluctuations and crises, thus increasing the reliability of mathematical models and econometric equations.

The Industrial Revolution shaped the 19th century, whereas in the 20th century, services played a similar role. This change was accompanied

---

[3]Mitchell, Wesley C. (1913).

by the financialisation of the economy, which gave rise to a new form to crises. Before the 20th century, a financial crisis could occur without economic agents noticing. Now, it propagates through the entire economy. Financial crises spread fast because global finance is a tightly interwoven system, as is global trade.

The crisis of 1929 began in the United States with the failure of the Bank of United States, a systemically important bank, whose defining characteristic was that it was too big to fail without bringing about the collapse of the financial system. The bank's grandiose name, suggesting it was an emanation of the state, meant that its failure reverberated around the world. In fact, this triggered what is considered to be the first major global crisis, reminiscent of contemporary crises. It was of exceptional magnitude and had devastating consequences, from which Europe has not yet fully recovered. It should be remembered that the Nazi rise to power, which led to the Second World War, was mainly due to widespread economic misery.

Similarly, the 2008 crisis, which began with the failure of another American bank, Lehman Brothers, unleashed a wave of populist sentiment. As Talleyrand explained in his memoirs, "the ranks of the discontented are made up of the thinking poor".[4]

There could have been a rescue of the two American banks. They were illiquid but not insolvent. In other words, despite having negative equity, these banks were not technically bankrupt. What they lacked were highly liquid assets to meet their immediate commitments. They were short of cash, a problem that a bridge loan could have solved. However, a bridge loan was not forthcoming from the United States regulator, which let them default and pushed them into bankruptcy. No one knows what would have happened if the government had arranged the loan to help them through this difficult period. In particular, wouldn't the cycle have caught up with developed economies in any case? Be that as it may, the whole world, especially Europe, paid a high price for the consequences of what, in many ways, was an inconsequential decision by the United States regulator.

Nowadays, crises have the characteristic of being global. Also, paradoxically, more damage is done to other countries than to the one where they originated. In other words, it is not the country triggering a global crisis that foots the bill. In the aftermath of a global crisis, there are no indemnities or reparations, as there might be after a war. The failings of

---

[4]Talleyrand-Périgord, Charles-Maurice (de). (2002).

American policymakers were responsible for the 1929 and 2008 crises taking on a devastating dimension, but other countries paid the price!

These failings — in a country that has produced the most Nobel prizes in economics — raise the question of why economics is not proving capable of providing policymakers with mistake-proofing tools. The word "crisis" is frequently used, not to say overused, in economic analysis. Whether the economic crisis is presented as global or sectoral, financial or affecting the real economy, the expression is nowadays pervasive to the point of suggesting that the phenomenon is permanent and has, therefore, become a normality, which is paradoxical.

Be that as it may, the mission of today's economists is to provide a theoretical explanation of its causes and the ensuing chain of events, as well as the means to mitigate its effects and prevent repetitions. Have they been successful? This question does indeed have to be asked, as it was raised in no uncertain terms by no less than the Queen of England, Elizabeth II. In November 2008, during the reception staged on the occasion of her visit to the prestigious London School of Economics (LSE), her Majesty asked her hosts:

"Why didn't anyone see the financial crisis coming?"

Slightly taken aback, her entourage quickly came up with a rather pat answer, adding that more time would be needed to provide her Majesty with a structured answer intelligible to non-economists.

In early 2009, the LSE decided to pursue the matter and respond with a reasoned argumentation to what is undoubtedly a challenge to economic science. There is no question of dodging the problem by settling for a few truisms. It therefore launched a call for contributions to answer Her Gracious Majesty's question without detour and, more broadly, to stem the tide of criticism directed at economists. Soon enough, the task of writing this reply was entrusted to three people. The first was Jim O'Neill, an English economist who was head of global economics research at Goldman Sachs. He gained notoriety with the publication of his seminal paper on the rise of emerging economies, in which he coined the acronym BRIC[5] for Brazil, Russia, India and China. The second was Tim Besley,

---

[5]BRICs in *Building Better Global Economic BRICs* was later modified to BRICS following the addition of South Africa. The BRICS concept has been widely adopted and gained institutional recognition, even though the five countries in question have enjoyed quite differing economic fortunes.

a professor at the LSE who was a rising star in British economics. The third was Nicholas MacPherson, the then permanent secretary to the British Treasury. He was the bearer of what economists call the "Treasury Opinion", the thoughts of senior British officials who were considered to be among the best economists in the world. Nicolas MacPherson studied at Oxford University's Balliol College, a venerable institution if ever there was one, as it boasts Adam Smith himself among its former students. The trio met regularly, often joined by William Keegan, the economic editor of the *Observer* newspaper, who acted as reporter.

This response took the form of a letter sent to Buckingham Palace in July 2009. Tim Besley did most of the legwork and wrote the bulk of the text. However, his paper was also vetted by the leading British economists at the British Academy Forum held on 17 June 2009.

After getting acquainted with the text, Her Majesty authorised the *Observer* to print a résumé. For the authors, the crisis is the consequence of an overly lax monetary policy and a refusal to correct current account imbalances on the part of both countries running deficits (such as the United States) and those running surpluses (China, Germany, Japan and the oil-producing countries).

But what is most interesting is the conclusion in the penultimate paragraph:

> "So in summary, Your Majesty, the failure to foresee the timing, extent and severity of the crisis and to head it off, while it had many causes, was principally a failure of the collective imagination of many bright people, both in this country and internationally, to understand the risks to the system as a whole".

Officially, faced with what is a worrying admission of impotence likely to bring the very function of economist into disrepute, there was no reaction from the Queen. Will the letter have dispelled Her Majesty's doubts? Probably not since these doubts were shared by an increasing number of people, including Paul Krugman. Shortly before the letter drafted by the LSE was delivered to Buckingham Palace, the influential British weekly *The Economist* published an article on 16 July 2009 in which it reported that, in a recent lecture, the winner of the 2008 Nobel Prize in Economics argued that much of the past 30 years of macroeconomics was "spectacularly useless at best, and positively harmful at worst".

Some three years later, while visiting the Bank of England in December 2012, the Queen indulged in some more or less ironic remarks, wondering if "people had got a bit [...] lax?" in the run-up to the 2009 crisis. The Financial Services Authority responded immediately, making their *mea culpa* and giving assurances that thinking about sound and prudent credit management had been, and remained, more than ever at the centre of their concerns.

Nevertheless, confessing to "a failure of the collective imagination" will not get economists off the hook forever. They must be aware of the need to respond in a practical, pragmatic way to the questions that have fuelled so much debate within the profession, as unanswered questions have an unsettling effect on all economic agents.

To better understand the explanations given to Her Majesty Queen Elizabeth II, let's first cast our minds back to the arguments of economists through the ages to then proceed to determine a theory of "crises".

Chapter 2

Theoretical Analysis of Crises

To find meaning in the notion of crisis and discern its relevance as precisely as possible, a definition is needed first of all, along with its contours. To do this, we must not talk exclusively about an "economic crisis" to avoid getting lost in the pursuit of theories about "crises of civilisation" or "crises of adolescence". Even if one limits the analysis to an "economic crisis", how does an "agricultural crisis", an "industrial crisis" or a "financial crisis" fit into the frame of things? The latter has become something of an umbrella term: the crisis of 2008–2009 is now systematically referred to as a "financial crisis". For the public at large, this term has the merit of identifying a guilty party traditionally held in rather low esteem.

Let us first agree on a definition.

Defining a crisis

To this end, let's first consider the entries in the *Dictionnaire de la langue française* by Émile Littré (commonly called simply the "Littré"):

> "Medical term. The turning point of a disease, announced by particular symptoms, such as abundant excretion, significant hemorrhaging, sweating, urinary deposits, etc. Happy crisis. Fatal crisis. Astrological opinion, falsely attributing an influence to the moon upon crises. Magnetic crisis, the name of the state into which magnetised people fall.

Figurative. A perilous or decisive moment. A crisis is in the offing. Business is in a state of crisis. A very dangerous political crisis.

Disturbance in production. Industrial or commercial crisis, disturbance, disruption of industrial operations or commercial transactions, suspending their execution. Financial crisis, considerable financial difficulties affecting public finances or business. Monetary crisis, financial difficulties resulting from the scarcity of money. Crises sometimes lead to higher prices for products, sometimes to lower prices. Wine crisis. Subsistence crisis.

Ministerial crisis, when a ministry is dissolved without being replaced.

Nature crisis, in reference to the great convulsions that occur on earth.

Etymology: from the Greek Κρίσις, "a decision", from κρίνειν, "to decide, judge"".

The Littré, which was first published in the 1870s, opens with the medical meaning of the term. It then departs from its literal use to its usage in figurative language, where the economy has pride of place.

Since the 19th century, the French term "crisis" has entered common usage as denoting a "disturbance of industrial operations or commercial transactions". Interestingly, in English texts referring to situations of this kind, "crisis" is not the immediate equivalent of the French term. The book by John Kenneth Galbraith [1908–2006] on the events of 1929 goes by the title *The Great Crash*, with crash normally denoting an "accident", and was translated into French as *La crise économique de 1929*. As for *The Return of Depression Economics and the Crisis of 2008* by Paul Krugman, it was translated as *Pourquoi les crises reviennent toujours*.

The generally held view is that Swiss historian and economist Jean Charles Léonard Simonde de Sismondi [1773–1842] was the first economist to systematically use the term "crisis". At a time when economics was largely dominated by French and English thinkers, "distress" was the term used to denote an economic situation characterised by unemployment and a contraction of activity. This departure from the literal use of the term can be traced to French economists, particularly Sismondi. Having witnessed firsthand the French Revolution, which his Swiss-born family fled, crisscrossing Europe before returning home to Geneva, Sismondi fell under the spell of Adam Smith's works. He was attracted by their positive content and spirit, in contrast to the violence and despair of

Jacobin politics in France. However, he found France under the Bourbon Restoration to be repugnant. Having wed a Welshwoman in 1819, he was appalled by the condition of the working class in his wife's country. In his *Nouveaux principes d'économie politique*, published in 1819, Sismondi broke with classical economists, developing a systematic critique of this school of economic thought. He contended that supply did not create sufficient demand, contrary to what has gone down in the annals as Say's law, named after the famous French economist who formulated it. There followed that, according to Sismondi, it was under-consumption, unbridled competition (leading to excessive falls in prices) and uncertainty that led to "crises", which would ultimately bring about the demise of the market economy. As for a solution, Sismondi advocated supporting demand.

To this end, Sismondi considered that there were three possible economic policies, which he described as follows:

(1) "Egyptian" consists of having the state shoulder a significant part of demand in the form of large works. With this proposition, Sismondi was one of the precursors of modern Keynesianism and one of the first thinkers to look into stimulus policies.
(2) "Sybarite" is based on a system for the distribution of purchasing power. For Sismondi, the central issue for an economy is that if firms increase wages, they increase their costs, reduce their profitability and ultimately go bankrupt. On the other hand, if firms maintain excessively low wages, there will be insufficient outlets for their goods. His proposition, therefore, was for the state to manage demand through an income policy based on large-scale redistribution using taxation. It is still all about stimulus, but this time acting on consumption.
(3) "Athenian" focuses on avoiding overproduction by reducing working time. This would encourage the development of culture and lead to, as in ancient Athens, the creation of places where citizens might congregate to exchange and discuss all manner of things.

The Panic of 1825 gave wide notice to Sismondi's theories about the economy's difficulty finding outlets for its production and the need for public action to mitigate the consequences of overproduction. In *The Communist Manifesto,* Karl Marx saluted Sismondi's criticism of capitalism, especially in Britain, where it had found its fullest expression. At the same time, the German philosopher dismissed the man as an exemplary representative of "petty-bourgeois socialism". Fundamentally, Marx criticised Sismondi for having conceived as a way out of the crisis of capitalism only a return to the idealised society of the 18th century, i.e. small towns where the elites gathered in learned academies and maintained harmonious commercial relations with a rural world, entertaining at long last the hope of staving off famines. Aside from the Sybarite, Egyptian and Athenian policy responses, Sismondi advocated above all a form of decentralised planning where collaboration between producers and consumers leads to the appropriate level of production.

Overproduction was central to Sismondi's analysis of capitalism and is intimately linked to what we might call an "industrial crisis". The very same idea sprung up at much the same time in the country at the forefront of the Industrial Revolution, namely Britain. One of the leading economists at the time, Thomas Malthus [1766–1834], also propounded theories about overproduction. Best known for his assertions about the calamitous consequences of a geometric progression of the population, the British economist and demographer was also one of the first to flag the possibility that demand might prove insufficient. For this reason, he was a virulent opponent of his French contemporary, Jean-Baptiste Say [1767–1832].

These first modern conceptions of a crisis in the context of a market economy start with the assertion that there can be a devastating gap between supply and demand. The cause must be either weak demand (underconsumption) or excess supply (overproduction). This systematic association of a crisis with a deficiency of demand was quick to elicit a response from the so-called classical economists, who were adamant in their belief that Say's law remained relevant. For them, supply creates its own demand. If a crisis occurs, its origin must be found elsewhere than in underconsumption or overproduction.

One of the first to tread this path was Pellegrino Rossi [1787–1848], who held the economic chair at the Collège de France from 1834 to 1840. He published a book, *Cours d'économie politique*, which to this day remains one of the most accessible and faithful exposés in French of the writings of British economist David Ricardo [1772–1823]. At a time when political economy in France was dominated by the heirs of Jean-Baptiste Say, Rossi popularised the theories of the English classical school. For him, demand is a complex mechanism of hierarchisation of needs in permanent adjustment, while supply displays a fair amount of inertia, adapting to demand but after a delay. Forces are released by the market, leading more to a dynamic disequilibrium than to a stable competitive equilibrium. To talk of a "crisis" to describe a constant and natural adaptation of the market and trade is therefore vain. Notwithstanding this adaptation, the economy does sometimes experience setbacks, serial failures, and population regression. The contention was that this should be interpreted as being the result of what nowadays we would term "exogenous shocks". Rossi talks of "uncertain ventures", referring to undertakings whose performances are not guaranteed. A crisis is created by the cumulative failure of these uncertain ventures. What might these be? Farming because of the vicissitudes of the weather; mining, for every pit is not rewarded with mineral in the desired form and abundance; and manufacturing, as new products are never assured of wooing the consumer. Rossi contends that "uncertain ventures" cannot be eradicated from the economic world, but that their number can be restricted and greater caution shown before taking up such economic undertakings, only to conclude that their total eradication cannot even be contemplated. He deduced from this the existence of "crises" that cannot be anticipated by anyone, that can rarely be corrected and whose timing will tend to be irregular.

Whether caused by deficient demand (endogenous shock) or sudden events beyond control (exogenous shock), much ink has been spilled about the "crisis" in economic literature, which convinced Charles Coquelin [1802–1852] to devote an article to this in his *Dictionnaire de l'économie politique*, published in 1854, which begins as follows:

"A commercial crisis is a sudden disturbance of business, which perturbs its progress and to a certain extent suspends its course. It ordinarily manifests itself in a sort of general discredit, leading to a depreciation of commercial values and public values, a suspension or slowdown of discounting by bankers, a glut of merchandise whose sales cease, and finally a more or less total stoppage of circulation. It always brings in its wake countless insolvencies. Bankruptcies multiply in commerce; the most financially distressed enterprises collapse, while those left standing incur considerable losses. Furthermore, as public funds undergo a depreciation corresponding to those affecting other stores of value, business failures are compounded by stock market disasters. A final consequence of this same phenomenon is that many workshops interrupt or slow their activity, leaving part of the workers out in the cold. Labour suffers and wages fall, rents decline, goods are sold at a loss or remain unsold; all classes of society are affected. While the crisis lasts, there is a kind of universal disarray.

This disturbance of business must be impermanent. Otherwise, it would not be a crisis but a chronic disease, implying a rapid ruin or at least a decline of the country affected by this disturbance.

Commercial crises, as just defined, seem to belong exclusively to modern times. They have been a frequent occurrence in Europe, especially in the present century, in England and France notably, becoming almost periodic. That is not to say that, in the past, commerce and industry did not suffer hugely from political upheavals, foreign or civil wars, and all manner of ills having plagued humanity, but the phenomenon did not suddenly break out in a violent and general explosion. On the contrary, it was felt by degrees, little by little, as the ravages of war and its manifold ills propagated. It often went much further than it commonly does nowadays, to the point of reducing populations to a state of destitution similar to that in which, as an exception to the rule, the population of unfortunate Ireland has found itself. It can thus be said with some confidence that commercial crises are a phenomenon particular to our time".

From this text emerge the following four key ideas that have nourished the reflections of economists and are still, in many respects, relevant and topical to this day:

(1) A "crisis" is a characteristic of the modern economy. Whereas problems that beset the rural economy were linked to the vagaries of nature, those affecting the industrial market economy (what was called the commercial economy in the 19th century) are linked to mechanisms specific to that economy. While the agricultural crisis is exogenous, the commercial crisis is endogenous.
(2) A crisis is defined as a contraction of economic activity affecting production as well as trade, the latter to be understood as per its current meaning.
(3) A crisis arises from a contraction of demand due to a credit crunch following excessive lending. More precisely, a crisis originates from the excesses of finance. This analysis prefigures, to some extent, that of the 20th- and 21st-century crises.
(4) A crisis is not permanent but cyclical. A country's structural difficulties are, in the words of Charles Coquelin, a "disease" that leads to its

wasting. On the other hand, while a crisis, though not fatal in essence, will eventually subside, it does tend to return regularly.

This last idea is important, for it begins to associate crises and cycles.

Is a crisis a phase in the cycle?

In 1913, in his seminal work entitled *Les crises périodiques de surproduction*, French economist Albert Aftalion [1874–1956] wrote that a "crisis is but one of the moments — in truth, the most distressing one — of an entire cycle taking place periodically".

The book was intended to be a critical analysis of the ideas of physician and statistician turned economist Clément Juglar, who rose to fame but then fell into obscurity, before his name was definitively associated with the theory of business cycles.

His father having left the Basses-Alpes (now the Alpes-de-Haute-Provence) for the capital, Clément Juglar was born in Paris on 15 October 1819. His father was a physician and intended for his son to follow in his footsteps. In 1836, Clément Juglar defended a thesis on the consequences of heart conditions on the lungs. This thesis is less remarkable for its medical qualities than for its abundant use of statistics, for the real passion of the young Juglar was quantitative analysis and numerical series. Having published well-documented articles on demography from 1846 onwards, it was the 1848 Revolution that sealed his future.

Initially enthusiastic, he was appalled at the turn of events. In particular, he questioned whether the claims of leading advocates of socialism, announcing that capitalism carried the seeds of its own destruction, had any basis in fact. As the increasing number of crises since the beginning of industrialisation, with their attendant unemployment and revolts, seemed to prove them right, Juglar sought to shed light on these claims and devoted 10 years to studying the main economies of his time. His findings were published in 1860 in an article which formed the basis of a book released in 1862 entitled *Des crises commerciales et leur retour périodique en France, en Angleterre et aux États-Unis*, in which he laid out the principle that there were economic cycles lasting between 9 and 10 years. His name survives in the term "Juglar cycle".

For Juglar, whose name is frequently associated with the medium-term cycle, the cycle originates in changes in the quantity of money in circulation due, in particular, to changes in the trade balance. As economic development differs from one country to another, some will generate a trade surplus. In these countries, the surplus results in an inflow of gold, increasing the money supply and causing inflation. This inflation leads to a loss of market share for the country's exports, ultimately resulting in a trade deficit. Gold flows out of the country, leading to deflation. The economic cycle is a monetary cycle that can be summarised as

$$\text{Trade Surplus} \rightarrow \text{Inflation} \rightarrow \text{Trade Deficit} \rightarrow \text{Deflation}$$

In this vision of the cycle, unemployment may rear its head. This occurs during the deflation phase and comes from the workers' refusal to accept lower wages. Once it is apparent that there will be no reduction in personal income, firms organise deflation through a reduction in payrolls, achieved by downsizing the workforce. The cycle then becomes one of alternating inflation and unemployment.

The success of Juglar's book and ideas was such that Léon Say [1826–1896], one of the grandsons of Jean-Baptiste Say and co-editor of the *Nouveau dictionnaire de l'économie politique*, the first version of which was published between 1889 and 1892, entrusted him with writing the article on "commercial crises".

Juglar wrote:

"As in diseases, a commercial crisis is a critical moment to go through. As soon as financial difficulties arise, the question is whether one will resist or one will succumb. A crisis is a touchstone that allows us to gauge the soundness of commercial houses, the size of their commitments and the resources they possess, in capital or in credit, to meet these. Thanks to the crisis, the market goes through a sort of selection; the houses that are out of sorts collapse; the others resist. This is how crises separate discredited houses from those that can be trusted. Carried away as people were on the wings of credit, they now touch ground once more, but alongside the businesses still standing, many more have been swept away. The crisis is therefore extremely short".

What emerges is that a crisis is an abnormal situation, notwithstanding its recurrence. There is also the idea that a crisis has a "Darwinian" dimension, providing the economic world with a mechanism of evolution based on natural selection and giving meaning to the dynamics of firms and the resulting economic growth. The crisis thus has losers and winners.

At much the same time, but on the other side of the Channel, William Stanley Jevons [1835–1882], one of the founders of neoclassical economics, came up with theories about market equilibrium. But what he observed was that during the 19th century, crises occurred at almost regular intervals (in 1825, 1836, 1848, 1857, 1866, 1873 and 1882, to be precise). He thus associated crises and cycles but gave an extra-economic climatic explanation for the origin of this process, to which we will return later. He completed his analysis with what, in his case too, was a Darwinian assessment. He wrote about a crisis that "the state of things is called a commercial collapse, because there is a sudden falling in of prices, credit and enterprise. It is also called a crisis, that is a dangerous and decisive moment [...] when it will soon be seen who is to become bankrupt, and who not".

Back in France, around much the same time as Albert Aftalion, Charles Gide [1847–1932], the first academic to lecture on economics at a French faculty from 1877 onwards, also associated crises and economic cycles.

In his book *Principes d'économie politique*, which contains his course material and was first published in 1898, he writes:

"The question of crises has been studied by economists of all countries with passionate — and, in our opinion, somewhat exaggerated — curiosity. It indeed involves all economic factors: production, consumption, credit, prices, savings, etc. But, because of the very complexity of all these facts, the explanations given are often contradictory and forecasts no less disappointing than those provided by meteorology".

He then provided his opinion:

"The word 'crisis' has a pathological signification. Crises may very well be likened to diseases of the economic organism, as they offer as varied characteristics as the innumerable ailments which afflict mankind. Some are short and violent, like attacks of fever, and manifest themselves by a high temperature followed by sudden depression; others are slow, 'like anaemia' — in the words of Emile de Laveleye.[1] Some are peculiar to

---

[1]A Belgian socialist economist, who has gone down in history for having given the first economics course in Belgium at the University of Liege in 1863.

one country; others are pandemics and spread around the world, like cholera. The word 'cycle' does not imply any idea of disorder or of disturbance. On the contrary, it conjures up the idea of rhythm. This is the law of this world, that of regularity in alternation, to which all phenomena of the physical order seem to be subject — not only the alternation of the seasons, but the barometric variations, the rise and fall of the glaciers, the precession of the equinoxes — and also those of the economic order, such as the balance of trade, the oscillations in the rate of interest, etc. There is nothing mysterious about this. There are only two possible states of affairs: immobility, which would be death, or oscillations around a position of equilibrium, which is life. From this perspective, it seems quite natural that all economic phenomena should take the form of a more or less regular wave line".

He insists:

"But above all, the most striking characteristic of crises is their periodicity. They follow one another with the regularity and majesty of a sea ball, each wave having an amplitude of about ten years, of which four or five years in ascending motion, four or five years in descending motion".

Charles Gide then sets out Jevons' own analysis:

"Such regularity could not be attributed to chance; it suggested the idea of some astronomical cycle. So we find Jevons turning to the skies for an explanation, and believing he had found it in the periodic recurrence of sunspots. At the time, the widely held view was that the maxima or minima of these spots occurred more or less every ten years. What might be the link between sunspots and crises? Well, the varying intensity of the sun's rays resulted in good or bad harvests, in turn determining crises. It would seem everything was considered in this cosmogonic novel".

For Jevons, it is not just the crisis but the cycle itself that is exogenous. Charles Gide mocked this "as mere romancing", even if today physicists and meteorologists have given some relevance to Jevons' point of view. His is an endogenous interpretation that inspires the solutions he advocates:

"If the cause of the crisis lies in the working class not having the means to increase its consumption to keep pace with the increase in production, the remedy should be sought in higher wages, or in a socialist regime which would assure the worker reaps the full product of his labour; or perhaps simply in a co-operative regime in which production, being organised only with a view to needs, and not with a view to profit, would not incite excessive and purely speculative overproduction.

If the cause of the crises lies in overcapitalisation, the banks will have to be relied upon, for they are the great and almost unique providers of credit. It is up to them to intervene at the right moment: either, when they see that the acceleration of circulation is becoming worrying, by raising the discount rate in order to tighten credit [...]; or, on the contrary, when the crisis is imminent, by rushing to rescue the houses that would be the first to go under and whose collapse would determine the general collapse.

Or the legislator must be the one to take preventive action, by controlling the issuance of securities by new companies or by regulating the futures markets.

In the latter case, however, the remedy is more doubtful. Here the evil is psychological rather than economic. It is rather a question of education; the public must be taught not to believe that because the price of a security is rising, it should be bought, nor that because it is falling, it should be sold.

Finally, if crises are seen as a natural, non-pathological phenomenon, a cyclical movement, then this begs the question of the usefulness of even seeking a remedy. Immobility is not a sign of life, and would a society in which there were no more highs and lows not risk becoming stuck in the stationary state predicted by Stuart Mill?"

In the classical vision of the economy, the economic dynamic is one of convergence towards market equilibrium. The neoclassical model, which became the reference from the 1870s onwards, is based on the notion of market equilibrium. At the macroeconomic level, the challenge for economists was to define a "general equilibrium", which was called "Walrasian" after its creator, the French economist Léon Walras [1834–1910]. There follows that, analysing the situation of the 19th century economy marked by successive periods of inflation and deflation, classical economists were led to develop a theory of crises and cycles that did not involve supply and demand dynamics and the equilibrium naturally resulting from the functioning of the competitive market. They therefore based the cycle on disturbance factors outside the economy and its regulation by the market. They remained of the view that the cycle and the crisis were exogenous phenomena.

For William Stanley Jevons (one of the leading neoclassical economists with Léon Walras), whose views on crises we have already discussed, the existence of cycles is directly linked to disturbances in the activity of the Sun. Basing his findings on the comparison between two series of data on the deformation of sunspots, on the one hand, and on the price of wheat, on the other, Jevons links cycles and the Sun. To do this, he performed one of the very first econometric calculations. At the time, the sunspot theory was ridiculed by his peers. However, it did launch the debate on the role of econometrics and the right way to use this analysis. Econometrics makes it possible to validate the observation of a correlation in the evolution of two variables. On the other hand, it does not explain the origin of this correlation: does it express a causal relationship, and if so, what is the cause and what is the effect? Does it express the fact that the two variables have a common cause, making them evolve simultaneously without one influencing the other? Or does it simply express a fortuitous situation in which the two variables evolve in parallel? In considering the conclusions reached by Jevons, experts had, for many years, chosen the third option and warned economists against jumping to conclusions that would transform an accidental correlation into a structural relationship. It so happens that Jevons' theses have since been borne out. By influencing the climate, solar activity does modify crop yields, inducing a cyclical evolution of agricultural production, which was still a determining factor in economic expansion at the time of Jevons' writings.

For Alfred Marshall [1842–1924], who trod in the footsteps of Jevons and went on to become one of the most influential economists of his time, there needed to be a more endogenous explanation for price cycles, even if it was still focused on agriculture. He argued that cycles arise from the time lag in the information available to players in certain markets, notably for agricultural commodities. The role of a price system is to transmit information to suppliers and buyers. In agriculture, the time between sowing and harvesting causes information distortion. The supplier reacts to the economic situation at sowing time, while the buyer does so when the harvest comes into sight. The market equilibrium model (when the quantity demanded is equal to the quantity supplied) can be formulated as follows:

$D(t) = ap(t) + b$ is the equation for demand, and $S(t) = cp(t-1) + d$ is the equation for supply. Bear in mind that demand declines as prices rise (reflected in the fact that "a" is negative) and supply increases as prices rise (reflected in the fact that "c" is positive).

Equality of supply and demand leads to the following equation: $ap(t) + b = cp(t-1) + d$, with the price series obtained being known in mathematics as an arithmetico–geometric series. If the absolute value given by c/a exceeds 1, the series has no finite limit, and there is never convergence, with prices following an erratic evolution that goes on amplifying, what Marshall termed a cycle.

For classical economists, the economic cycle is either linked to production conditions in agriculture or to international distortions in productivity. Distortions are ultimately lessened by the competition brought about by free trade policies. The reference in this matter is the Juglar cycle. Beyond its foreign trade dimension, it reflects above all monetary problems. Despite the unemployment associated with it, its practical translation is a sinusoidal evolution of prices.

From this intellectual journey to define a crisis and its links with the cycle, what can be seen is that, as early as the 19th century, a crisis was denoted by a contraction in economic activity (or negative growth, if you prefer). A crisis has a financial component that is decisive. It is cyclical and not structural, though there are losers and winners, and thus contributes to structural changes.

1929 crisis: Keynes takes the stage

The crisis that shook the global economy after the Wall Street Crash of October 1929 led economists to expand, even reformulate, their theoretical approach. Two names symbolise this new school of economic thought.

The first was Irving Fisher [1867–1947]. Having shown a particular talent and inclination for mathematics, he graduated and then received his first PhD in economics from Yale, teaching economics at this university until his retirement and publishing three seminal works: *Capital and Investment* (1906), *Quality Theory of Money* (1911) and *The Theory of Interest: As Determined by the Impatience to Spend Income and*

Opportunity to Invest It (1930).[2] Another book by Irving Fisher, *Booms and Depressions: Some First Principles* (1933),[3] opens with a quote from British banker and economist Sir Josiah Stamp: "Money, as a physical medium of exchange, made a diversified civilisation possible [...] And yet it is money, in its mechanical more than in its spiritual effects, which may well, having brought us to the present level, actually destroy society".

Irving Fisher defines depression as a condition in which businesses become unprofitable.

He explains that if an individual debtor has not borrowed enough, he can easily correct the error by borrowing more. If the debtor has gone too far into debt, especially if he has misjudged as to maturity dates, he may find himself caught in a trap. He will try to put off the day when he has to pay his debt by refunding for as long as possible. Governments accomplish this by rolling over their debt. This can be far trickier for an individual or a firm, with creditors having more limited refinancing capacity over time.

For Irving Fisher, of the nine factors leading to great depressions, over-indebtedness is the most potent: it occurs during a period of strong growth due to major innovations, during which expectations of profits are extremely elevated. The first three factors also include the currency-volume factor and the price-level factor. All three factors are closely locked together when there is a market reversal, triggering the start of a vicious spiral into depression.

The theory of economic crises developed by Irving Fisher can be applied not just to the 1929 crisis but also to the 2000 dot-com bubble and the 2008 subprime mortgage crisis. Mortgage product innovation led to subprime mortgage securitisation, creating complex products initially intended for a niche market before the United States banks rolled them out worldwide. Such was the complexity and opacity of these banking products that investors relied exclusively upon the assessments of the United States credit rating agencies to determine their value. When it became clear that the estimates produced by these US-only, government-sponsored agencies did not hold water, there was a market reversal. Banks were forced to freeze prices for their funds, as the lack of liquidity made it impossible to fairly value the underlying the United States asset-backed

---

[2]This work includes another book written by Fisher, Irving (1907).
[3]Fisher, Irving (1933).

securities. On 9 August 2007, BNP Paribas suspended the calculation of net asset value for three funds. Panic spread among creditors and debtors, triggering the crisis.

As explained by Irving Fisher, distress selling and a stampede of liquidation by borrowers are then followed by a contraction of the deposit currency through a decrease in velocity, the effect being to lower the general price level.

Upon the first three main factors — debt, currency volume and price level — locking together during a market reversal, the six other oscillating factors identified by Irving Fisher are as follows:

(1) net worth,
(2) profit,
(3) production,
(4) psychology,
(5) currency turnover,
(6) the rates of interest.

Thus, after the liquidation of debts, the contraction of the deposit currency and the ensuing decline in the general price level, the business net worth shrinks and sometimes turns into failure and bankruptcy. There is an inexorable decline in profits and, ultimately, in production. This drives up unemployment and drives down trade. This dynamic will erode confidence, leading to the slowing of currency (i.e. slower velocity of circulation) and its hoarding. This leads to lower money interest but higher real interest.[4]

Irving Fisher noted that, to translate money interest into real interest, it is necessary to take account of at least two points in time, namely the time when the debt is contracted and the time (or times) when it is repaid. The United States economist also pointed out that while the nine main factors are set forth in a good pedagogical order, it is not strictly chronological, as "a depression may be said to be full of tangles and cross-currents".[5]

For Irving Fisher, the guilty party is the one who triggered this vicious circle in which individuals, businesses and banks engage in a race for liquidity. In the words of playwright Eugène Ionesco, "Take a circle, caress it, and it will turn vicious". The guilty party is the one that took the

---

[4] *Ibid.*
[5] *Ibid.*, p. 41.

circle, setting the process in motion. Unproductive debts are the initial problem. What signals the start of a depression is a lowering of the general price level.

In its original meaning, deflation refers to the release of air. In reference to currency or economic situations, from 1916, it can be defined as:

> "An economic phase during which there is a general and lasting decline in the price level of goods and services. During deflation, the purchasing power of currency rises over time. This can therefore be an incentive to defer consumption and investment, in turn leading to an economic slowdown. It is generally characterised by a reduction in margins, with firms cutting costs as much and as fast as needed to keep pace with the decline in their activities. Finally, this is a period of difficulty for indebted firms, as deflation automatically accentuates debt burdens".[6]

For Irving Fisher, deflation is "the root of almost all the evils".[7] He made the point that if the liquidation of debts were prevented from bulging the purchasing power of the dollar, i.e. if the dollar were safeguarded, the chain of events mentioned above (except for the change in money interest) would be forestalled, and the consistency between money interest and real interest would be preserved. If so, there would be no depression, simply a disturbance in the debts themselves and in their money interest.

However, the liquidation of debts will not go on forever. Over time, this process will reduce not only the number of remaining debts but also their real size. Every business failure, bankruptcy and reorganisation speeds up liquidation by striking off a part of the debts. Moreover, the reduction in the volume of trade caused by the fall in prices tends to check that fall. Through real liquidation and/or failures and a diminution of trade, the bottom of the descending spiral will finally be reached. The time comes when the business world is left in a state of under-indebtedness. For Irving Fisher, the debt cycle will then be at zero hour, ready for a recovery that may merge again into a boom phase, similar to the one enjoyed previously, and a prelude to a new vicious circle.

Irving Fisher said he thought he had found the "main secret"[8] of depressions — at least of many depressions. In his view, this secret lies in

---

[6] Vernimmen, Pierre (2022).
[7] Fisher, Irving (1933). *Op. cit.*, p. 39.
[8] *Ibid.*, p. 26.

the link he found between the effects of deflation and over-indebtedness. When over-indebtedness goes so far that the resulting mass liquidation defeats itself, there is a paradox that explains what he calls the "mystery" of many depressions.

Broadly, economic growth creates a climate of confidence, which encourages economic agents to take more risks and, consequently, to take on more debt. This is what, when they try to repay their debts, causes a fall in the general price level, which in turn is responsible for an increase in the weight of debt in the economy. When this happens, liquidation doesn't really liquidate. The depression goes right on until there are sufficient failures or bankruptcies to wipe out the activating cause — the debts. Irving Fisher considers that this vicious circle is at the origin not only of the 1929 crisis (which he did not foresee, although in the 1920s he was considered the oracle of Wall Street, and which ruined him) but also of many depressions.

The main conclusion reached by Irving Fisher in *Booms and Depressions* is that depressions can, for the most part, be prevented thanks to a definite policy in which the Federal Reserve System must play an important role.[9]

The second economist to have gained prominence from the revision of economic theories in the wake of the 1929 crisis was John Maynard Keynes [1883–1946]. Chapter 22 of *The General Theory of Employment, Interest, and Money* is devoted to the trade cycle and the phenomenon of the crisis.

What is important in the analysis of the trade cycle and crisis in this book is that Keynes looked at these in the context of the functioning of the real economy and concluded that they were not due to an excess of money and overabundance of credit but to a sudden collapse in the marginal efficiency of investment ("marginal efficiency of capital" was the term coined by Keynes for this phenomenon). In contrast to Irving Fisher, Keynes considers that fiscal policy, not monetary policy, should guide the actions of the authorities.

Keynes writes:

"I can best introduce what I have to say by beginning with the later stages of the boom and the onset of the 'crisis'. We have seen above that the marginal efficiency of capital depends, not only on the existing abundance or scarcity of capital goods and the current cost of production

---

[9] *Ibid.*

of capital goods, but also on current expectations as to the future yield of capital goods. In the case of durable assets it is, therefore, natural and reasonable that expectations of the future should play a dominant part in determining the scale on which new investment is deemed advisable. But, as we have seen, the basis for such expectations is very precarious. Being based on shifting and unreliable evidence, they are subject to sudden and violent changes. It is often convenient in contexts where there is no room for misunderstanding to write 'the marginal efficiency of capital', where 'the schedule of the marginal efficiency of capital' is meant".[10]

The crisis is the consequence of a collapse in the marginal efficiency of capital and its expansion through investment. The response to the crisis is natural. It lies in maintaining the volume of investment and improving its content by substituting public investment for private investment. The crisis ceases to be monetary, requiring states to respond by increasing investment spending.

Of all Keynes's disciples, the one who took this logic the furthest, expressing his belief that states were capable, if not of avoiding, at least of containing crises, was probably Walter Heller [1915–1987].

Eventually serving as chair of the Department of Economics at the University of Minnesota, Walter Heller helped forge the modern tools of economic analysis, such as the notions of potential GDP and full-employment surplus (or deficit), to which we will return later. He established himself as the great theorist of fiscal policy, which he made the central element of all economic regulation and which, according to him, made it possible to render the very notion of crisis obsolete. Fiscal policy acts structurally through spending and must be used in particular to launch a "war on poverty". And it acts cyclically through fiscal policy. Adopting a clear-cut view of the famous Phillips trade-off between inflation and unemployment, he considered that taxes should be lowered in times of unemployment and raised in times of inflation. If taxation places reliance on "automatic stabilisers", so that tax receipts are directly linked to the economic situation, this makes it possible to achieve this result without any deliberate action by the public authorities. Confronted in the 1970s by stagflation, featuring both high inflation and unemployment, he honed his

---

[10]Keynes, John Maynard (1936), Chapter 22.

vision of fiscal policy, his view being that personal income taxes needed to be increased to contain inflation, while corporate income taxes needed to be reduced to encourage investment and combat unemployment.

The Keynesian legacy also includes a financial aspect. For Keynes, the crisis of the 1930s went beyond the simple cycle and took on a dramatic dimension due to the financial elements. His hypothesis of financial instability was systematised in particular by Hyman Minsky [1919–1996]. In 1986, the American economist published *Stabilizing an Unstable Economy*, which was in the post-Keynesian tradition, although he made it clear in the preface that being post-Keynesian did not mean being slavishly dependent on the works of the "Great Man".[11] The notion of the "Minsky moment" was introduced in this book. According to this theory, each crisis, such as the one in 1929, is preceded by a "Minsky moment", corresponding to a phase of financial euphoria and ill-considered economic optimism, marked by increasing inequality and exploding debt and dominated by wilfully blind economic actors who refuse to contemplate the very idea of the ruptures that are coming.

Minsky also states that:

> "The major flaw of our type of economy is that it is unstable. This instability is not due to external shocks or to the incompetence or ignorance of policy-makers. Instability is due to the internal processes of our type of economy. The dynamics of a capitalist economy which has complex, sophisticated, and evolving financial structures leads to the development of conditions conducive to incoherence — to runaway inflation or deep depressions. But incoherence need not be fully realised because institutions and policy can contain the thrust to instability. We can, so to speak, stabilise instability".[12]

In contrast to Allan Greenspan, the chairman of the Federal Reserve from 1987 to 2006, who declared that "there is nothing involved in federal regulation per se which makes it superior to market regulation", Hyman Minsky considered that "finance cannot be left to free markets".[13] He also declared that "in a world with capitalist finance it is simply not true that

---

[11] Minsky, Hyman P. (1986).

[12] *Ibid.*, p. 11.

[13] *Ibid.*, p. 324.

the pursuit by each unit of its own self-interest will lead an economy to equilibrium. [...] Supply and demand analysis — in which market processes lead to an equilibrium — does not explain the behaviour of a capitalist economy, for capitalist financial processes mean that the economy has endogenous destabilizing forces".[14]

Formalisation of cycle post-1929: Hansen and Samuelson provide another conception of Keynes's general theory

For the Keynesian economists who dominated the 20th century, it was necessary to reformulate the cycle theory to explain the mechanism of crises. The cycle thus revisited finds its origin neither in factors acting at the margins of the economy, nor in the monetary situation, but in the functioning of production. The cycle cannot be a price cycle, insofar as Keynesians argue that prices are somewhat rigid. The economic translation of the cycle and its measurement concern changes in quantities: quantity produced through the change in growth, and quantity mobilised to achieve this production through the change in employment and unemployment. In place of Juglar's classical vision of inflation alternating with deflation, Keynesians substitute a vision in which periods of strong growth marked by tensions on production capacities alternate with periods of unemployment and capital underutilisation.

The transition between the two versions of the cycle was provided by Albert Aftalion [1874–1956], who taught not only economics but also statistics at Lille University and then Paris University. In his book *Les crises périodiques de surproduction* published in 1913, the French economist explicitly links crises and cycles. He explains economic fluctuations using what is called the "real sphere" of the economy, namely business investment. In order to represent this mechanism, Aftalion used the stove metaphor. What is this?

If a room has a stove and a window and its occupants complain about the cold, the immediate reaction is to stoke up the stove. Since coal is slow to ignite, there is a tendency to overfill. As a result, when the fire gets going, the room will become unbearably hot. The reaction is to open the window to let in outside air, bringing the room back to its original

---

[14]*Ibid.*, p. 280.

temperature. And so on. [...] Similarly, in the economy, businesses, seeing reserves of purchasing power, invest. In doing so, they increase not only production capacity but also demand, which deceives them about the reality of the opportunities existing in the economy and encourages them to amplify the investment dynamic. As a result, after a while, the economy faces a glut of machinery. Drawing on the stove metaphor, Aftalion refers to this as "overheating", a term that has stuck to describe periods of excessive economic growth driven by overly high levels of investment.

According to this theory, it is the inertia of business and its blindness to the real capital needs of the economy that cause the crisis. While cutting investment spending allows a return to a better situation by reining back capital to a level consistent with reality, it also heightens the crisis by reducing the outlets for industries producing capital goods.

The possible response of economic policy can be deduced from the stove metaphor. Monetary policy is the window in the room. It can be opened to cool down the room, which amounts to tightening monetary policy by raising interest rates when the economy is overheating. The window can be closed when the room is too cold, but this is not entirely effective. In the same way, monetary policy is the right tool for curbing inflation and cooling an overheating economy but is relatively ineffective in reviving (warming up) a moribund economy. Fiscal policy is like putting coal in the stove. But it has a limit, which is the content of the coal scuttle. Coal symbolises the state's borrowing capacity, which Aftalion took as not being unlimited.

It was an American economist, in the person of John Maurice Clark [1884–1963], who disseminated Aftalion's ideas in the English-speaking world. He did so all the more willingly, for he shared Aftalion's liking for original and rather heterodox economists. He coined the term "accelerator effect" to denote the relationship between fixed investment and economic growth. This contends that fixed investment sustains economic growth, which in turn drives up fixed investment, with the latter moving towards its desired value faster and faster with respect to time.

It is in Chapter 22 of *The General Theory of Employment, Interest and Money* that Keynes establishes the link between the trade cycle and the phenomenon of the crisis. In his notes on the trade cycle, Keynes explains that:

"Since we claim to have shown in the preceding chapters what determines the volume of employment at any time, it follows, if we are right, that our theory must be capable of explaining the phenomena of the Trade Cycle. If we examine the details of any actual instance of the Trade Cycle, we shall find that it is highly complex and that every element in our analysis will be required for its complete explanation. In particular we shall find that fluctuations in the propensity to consume, in the state of liquidity-preference, and in the marginal efficiency of capital have all played a part. But I suggest that the essential character of the Trade Cycle, and, especially, the regularity of time-sequence and of duration which justifies us in calling it a cycle, is mainly due to the way in which the marginal efficiency of capital fluctuates".[15]

Keynes links the crisis and the trade cycle to changes in fixed investment, drawing directly on the theory of investment expounded by Albert Aftalion and John Maurice Clark.

The investment accelerator effect is the foundation of the Keynesian approach to the cycle. This is expressed in the Hansen–Samuelson oscillator model, which is both simple and sophisticated. This model was developed by Paul Samuelson [1915–2009], who ascribed the model mainly to Alvin Hansen, his mentor in the days of its creation. Alvin Hansen [1887–1975] was an American economist who served notably as President Truman's economic adviser.

The model describes an economy with no external sector and no state, since the model purports to demonstrate that the cycle is not due to international trade or to blunders in the conduct of economic policy. Four equations are formulated: two traditional accounting equations and two theoretical equations, each corresponding to different moments in the economic process:

Accounting equations:
(1) Equality between supply and demand: $Y(t) = C(t) + I(t)$
where t designates the period of reference;
(2) Say's law, i.e. N. Gregory Mankiw's 8th Principle of Economics: $Y(t) = R(t)$.
Theoretical equations:
(1) *Consumption function*: $C(t) = cR(t - 1)$;
(2) *Investment function*: $I(t) = a [R(t - 1) - R(t - 2)]$.

[15]Keynes, John Maynard (1936).

In the investment function, the level of investment depends exclusively on a firm's expected opportunities from the observed growth in aggregate income. It does not consider the impact of interest rate levels on investment and makes equality between savings and investment a simple matter of fact. This harks directly back to the relationship between investment and growth put forward by John Maurice Clark.

Combining the four equations, the evolution of output over time must satisfy the following equation:

$$Y(t) - (c + a)\, Y(t - 1) + a\, Y(t - 2) = 0$$

This mathematical problem is solved by considering the so-called associated characteristic equation, which is of the form:

$$x^2 - (c + a)\, x + a = 0$$

If the discriminant $(c + a)^2 - 4a$ of this second-degree equation is negative, the solution is a trigonometric line in time, so that the output can be expressed as a periodic function. Solving the model gives a solution that can be written as a function of time in the form

$$Y(t) = Y0 \ a \ \cos\omega t$$

The investment mechanism formulated as depending exclusively on opportunities expected by firms leads to the appearance of an economic cycle. In this context, unemployment can be analysed, not as a lasting problem of the economy, but as associated with a transitory phase followed by a boom, leading to a resolution of underemployment.

To extend this model, the view is that the economy oscillates around a trend that can be defined as potential growth. This trend, i.e. the potential output of the economy, is a function of technical progress, available outlets for capital and in particular the organisation of work and the change in the active population. In the Hansen–Samuelson model, the trend is given by a, i.e. the reaction of investment to the change in demand.

Experts have come to define for each economy its potential GDP. The growth rate is then broken down into three components: the change in this measure of GDP, i.e. the potential growth rate; the cyclical component that results in real GDP being on occasion higher (positive output gap) and on occasion lower (negative output gap) than potential GDP; and noise, or if you prefer, an irregular component, that generally leads to a contraction of GDP following exogenous shocks.

The Hansen–Samuelson oscillator model cannot purport to describe the situation of a country perfectly because it gives too restrictive a view of investment motives and because, in its construct, changes in production, given the cosine shape, would return negative values. This model aims to be heuristic, providing an understanding of the economy's cyclical dimension but not describing the totality of the productive process. One of its merits is that it provides a mathematical framework for the consequences of the economic agents' different perceptions of the situation over time. It therefore goes beyond Marshall's agricultural model. Time-varying perceptions lead to a linear relationship between the different values of an economic variable over time. In the case of the Hansen–Samuelson oscillator, the variable in question is GDP, with the relation being established between three moments.

This method can be generalised by mobilising more than three moments. In particular, the modern mathematical analysis of growth leads to a four-period relation between the different values of output. What algebra shows is that when a linear relationship is established between different values in time of a variable, to find the mode of expression of such a variable as a function of time, one must associate a polynomial called the characteristic polynomial. When four periods are used, the polynomial is of degree three. Given the fundamental theorem of algebra, also known as the d'Alembert–Gauss theorem, the characteristic polynomial has a set of roots, i.e. numbers cancelling it, which are either real numbers or complex numbers. This mathematical outcome makes it possible to isolate, through this polynomial's real and complex roots, phenomena with an exponential profile, on the one hand, and phenomena with a sinusoidal profile, on the other hand. The Hansen–Samuelson oscillator is the simplest form of this outcome since the characteristic polynomial is a second-degree trinomial. However, the method it uses can be applied to various economic variables, determining changes in each one associating a trend, corresponding to the real roots of the characteristic polynomial, and a cycle, corresponding to the complex roots of this polynomial. In particular, when this model is generalised to a characteristic polynomial of the third degree, it automatically generates a trend corresponding to its real root and a cycle corresponding to its two possible complex roots.

Be that as it may, there are limitations to the Hansen–Samuelson oscillator model, not in the application of its mathematical reasoning, but in the fact that the model is based on two extreme assumptions:

- The first is the assumption of total price rigidity, so that the response to any change in the business environment is a change in the quantity produced.
- The second assumption is that investment depends exclusively on the firms' expected opportunities. These expectations are based on changes in past growth and correspond to a vision of the economy in which equality between savings and investment is reduced to a simple accounting observation, with no economic implications.

Nevertheless, one can draw three conclusions from this model:

- The regulating element, explaining not only economic growth but also its fluctuations, is investment. This is where the focus of economic policy should be.
- The economy is cyclical. Real GDP goes through phases when it is higher than potential GDP and periods when it is lower. The difference between potential and actual GDP is called the output gap. Economic growth can therefore be traced to potential growth, namely the change in potential GDP and which corresponds to the real root of the characteristic polynomial mentioned above, a cyclical component corresponding to its complex roots and, finally, an irregular component triggering crises that can be termed "exogenous crises".
- The economy alternates between phases of inflation and unemployment, the latter being a reformulation of what economists know as the "Phillips trade-off". For some, this corresponds to N. Gregory Mankiw's 10th Principle of Economics.

Currently the Robert M. Beren Professor of Economics at Harvard University, N. Gregory Mankiw is the author of the *Principles of Economics*, a textbook that has become a global reference. The book introduces the following 10 principles of economics:

(1) People face trade-offs.
(2) The cost of something is what you give up to get it.
(3) Rational people think at the margin.

(4) People respond to incentives.
(5) Trade can make everyone better off.
(6) Markets are usually a good way to organise economic activity.
(7) Governments can sometimes improve market outcomes.
(8) A country's standard of living depends on its ability to produce goods and services.
(9) Prices rise when the government prints too much money.
(10) Society faces a short-run trade-off between inflation and unemployment.[16]

Commenting on the 10th Principle of Economics, Mankiw defined the business cycle as "irregular and largely unpredictable fluctuations in economic activity, as measured by the production of goods and services or the number of people employed". In this context, the cycle is the observation of alternating periods of inflation and unemployment, while the crisis is the moment in this cycle when the growth of the economy falters and unemployment rises as a result.

He defines the crisis, which, as would any self-respecting Anglo-Saxon, he terms a recession, as the most unfavourable moment in the business cycle, marked by two consecutive quarters of contraction in economic activity. This pretty much corresponds to the definition given by the French National Institute of Statistics and Economic Studies (Institut National de la Statistique et des Études Économiques, INSEE), which is that a recession is a "period of temporary economic decline during which trade and industrial activity are reduced, generally identified by a fall in GDP in two successive quarters".

Real business cycle theory

Formulated in a 1982 paper by the economists Finn E. Kydland and Edward C. Prescott, the winners of the 2004 Nobel Prize in Economic Sciences, this theory postulates that bouts of slower growth or recessions are due to sudden falls in productivity caused by exogenous shocks, such as the 1973 oil shock. The two economists dismissed the idea that monetary policy influenced these phenomena, with their view being that the

---

[16]Mankiw, Gregory N. and Taylor, Mark P. (2017).

duration and magnitude of the crisis depended on the firms' degree of reactivity and their capacity to increase their investments and redirect them towards the new needs revealed by the shock.

Their point of view was developed by Charles Plosser in a 1989 paper that set out the theses of what has since been called the Real Business Cycle School (RBCS). The main thrust of the RBCS approach is that contemporary analyses of crises are driven by exclusively macroeconomic considerations, giving excessive importance to economic policy decisions, particularly monetary policy.

In reality, crises come back to shake the economy irregularly and are linked to shocks and decisions by various economic agents. Understanding crises requires a microeconomic analysis, based on the idea that each economic agent has a clear and simple objective, which is the maximisation of profit in the case of the firm and well-being in the case of the consumer.

The mathematical translation of this view is that, in the Hansen–Samuelson oscillator model, the characteristic polynomial associated with the model has no complex roots. As a result, the economy is the result of a trend and an irregular component. It is this randomness that defines the crisis and its distribution over time that allows the word "cycle" to be used. In this sense, for these economists, the 2009 recession has nothing to do with the collapse of Lehman Brothers, which shook the financial world but cannot explain the difficulties of the automobile industry. On the other hand, just as the 1975 recession was caused by a quadrupling of the price of oil, so is the 2009 recession linked to the fact that 2008 witnessed a third oil shock, with the price of a barrel of oil hitting $141.23 on 1 July 2008.

Crises herald permanent transformations: Regulation theory

Born in the early 1970s, the regulation[17] theory was and still is championed by several French economists. For its proponents, the description of a country's economic difficulties as a "temporary" downturn, as the

---

[17]Defined as the compound effects of diverse mechanisms on the economy as a whole, given the existing economic structures and social framework. Boyer, Robert (1986).

INSEE definition of a recession suggests, simply will not do. For them, a crisis does not last two or three quarters but constitutes a long phase of transition between two forms of organisation of the market economy that they call "capitalism", in a tradition harking back to Marxism. Two major books mark the contribution of regulation theorists to the economic debate: *Accumulation, Inflation, Crises* by Robert Boyer and Jacques Mistral, published in 1978, and *Économie politique des capitalismes* by Robert Boyer, published in 2015, whose qualifying subtitle could not be more explicit, being the theory of regulation and crises.

In this book, Robert Boyer, referring to the Marxist tradition, states that "regulation theory is part of this tradition, but it intends to amend and extend the analyses of Capital, both in the light of the modern methods of the economist and thanks to the lessons resulting from the transformation of capitalism since the end of the nineteenth century".[18]

The key word in the approach of regulation theorists is "Fordism". This term refers to an economy in which growth is driven by the redistribution of productivity gains to wage earners in the form of regular pay increases. This redistribution leads to an increase in demand, justifying a regular flow of investments and ensuring robust growth. However, since the end of the "Glorious Thirty", considered by proponents of the regulation theory as the pinnacle of "Fordism", the capitalist system has been in crisis.

Unable to restore the efficiency characterising Fordism, the leaders of the developed countries have kept changing their economic policies and organisation, alternating between nationalisation and privatisation, stimulus policies and austerity policies, trade liberalisation and championing economic patriotism.

Despite these repeated changes in strategy, governments have been unable to restore high growth rates. For France, potential growth, which was 5.5% in the 1960s, is now below 1%. It is this phenomenon that deserves the name of crisis. In contrast to the real business cycle theory, the regulation theory contends that the economy is in a permanent state of crisis. This is a visceral crisis of a system — capitalism. It stems from the approximations of decision-makers, which in turn arise from conflicts and confrontations between social groups and from contradictions in the interests of the different economic agents.

---

[18]Boyer, Robert (2022).

The system is in a kind of permanent crisis inasmuch as it is unable to achieve full employment and price stability. In the 1970s, there was the misguided belief that inflation would maintain a high growth rate and thus full employment. When this model failed, it led to the assertion of the need to combat inflation in the 1980s, restoring the power of savers and shareholders but creating a high level of unemployment, mainly among the least skilled segments of the population.

The crisis reflects the intrinsic weakness of institutions, becoming the prelude to the emergence of a new system which, for years, regulatory economists have believed could only be socialist in order to be stable. To quote Robert Boyer, regulation theory is between "Marxist tradition and historical institutionalism". Drawing a line under the nostalgia surrounding the "Glorious Thirty" of the regulation school, the same Robert Boyer writes: "It is clear that Fordism was atypical with regard to the regimes that preceded it and those that may succeed it".[19]

---

[19] *Ibid.*, p. 355.

Chapter 3

Economic Cycle and Policy

By identifying the change in private investment as the origin of the cycle, the Hansen–Samuelson oscillator implicitly provides a means of smoothing the cycle. It is necessary and sufficient to modify the volume of public investment to maintain the total volume of investment constant. Consequently, fiscal policy imposed itself as the policy tool to cushion the impact of the cycle and contain the crisis.

Fiscal policy comes into play

The multiplier model is an expression of the effectiveness of fiscal policy. The multiplier mechanism can be described as follows. R is a country's total income. The part consumed is cR, where the coefficient c is the propensity to consume. It is less than one, as the additional consumption cannot be greater than the additional income itself. Now, suppose that the government increases its spending, i.e. G, by dG without offsetting this additional spending by raising additional taxes. The government's suppliers will receive dG, passing this on to their employees, who consume part of this amount, or more precisely, cdG. The merchant receiving this amount will in turn spend part of this amount, $c(cdG)$, by making purchases from other merchants. They in turn will spend $c(c^2dG)$, and so on and so forth. In this sequence, the final total spending is equal to dG spent by the state and $cdG + c^2dG + c^3dG + \cdots + c^ndG + \cdots$ spent by individuals.

There follows that total demand increases by dG $(1 + c + c^2 + c^3 + \cdots + c^n + \cdots)$, i.e. $dG/(1 - c)$. The government having injected dG into the economic circuit, and the additional demand being $dG/(1 - c)$, this means that the multiplier is $(1/(1 - c))$.

When based on the vision of the Keynesian cycle and the functioning of the multiplier effects, the management of public finances will rely on the so-called automatic stabilisers, without direct intervention by policymakers. In this approach, policymakers will be asked to approve spending budgets that will adjust themselves at the same rates as potential GDP and, therefore, at the economy's potential growth rate. Concurrently, taxation needs to be based exclusively on changes in income to ensure that tax receipts are directly proportional to real GDP. Finally, government spending and receipts must be structured in such a way that there is a fiscal equilibrium when real GDP is in line with potential GDP. Under these conditions, the economy will overheat when real GDP exceeds potential GDP, with tax receipts therefore exceeding government spending. Symmetrically, economic slowdowns correspond to periods of lower tax receipts, creating fiscal deficits and thus enabling a reduction in Keynesian unemployment. Management of the cycle relying on automatic stabilisers means that it is the reduction in taxes that serves to stimulate the economy.

When management is based on automatic stabilisers, this is what is termed a countercyclical policy. In the conduct of fiscal policy, it leads to the identification of the structural deficit as distinct from the cyclical deficit.

The structural deficit is a deficit that subsists when real GDP becomes equal to potential GDP. The cyclically adjusted balance (CAB) refers to the fiscal surplus or fiscal deficit adjusted for fluctuations linked to the economic cycle. The cyclical deficit is the deficit that can be attributed to these fluctuations. How do you calculate cyclical and structural deficits in practice?

The approach assumes that automatic stabilisers are at play, so the delta for G is the same as for potential GDP (Pot), and the delta for T is the same as for real GDP (Pre). Δ is the total deficit, which breaks down into a structural deficit (Δs) and a cyclical deficit (Δc). The starting point is a balanced budget where $\Delta s = 0$.

When α is the tax burden rate,

$$T = \alpha\text{Pre}$$

When Pre = Pot, then

$$G = T = \alpha\text{Pre} = \alpha\text{Pot}$$

As the cycle unfolds, this means that

$$\Delta c = G - T = \alpha \text{Pot} - \alpha \text{Pre} = \alpha(\text{Pot} - \text{Pre})$$
$$= \alpha \times \text{output gap}$$

The cyclical deficit is therefore equal to the output gap multiplied by the tax burden rate. The structural deficit is the difference between the total deficit and the cyclical deficit.

European treaties draw distinctions between the two types of fiscal deficits and impose different requirements on each. The Treaty on Stability, Coordination and Governance in the Economic and Monetary Union (TSCG), adopted by France in 2012, stipulates in Article 3 that:

"(a) the budgetary position of the general government of a Contracting Party shall be balanced or in surplus;

(b) the rule under point (a) shall be deemed to be respected if the annual structural balance of the general government is at its country-specific medium-term objective, as defined in the revised Stability and Growth Pact, with a lower limit of a structural deficit of 0.5% of the gross domestic product at market prices; [...]

(d) where the ratio of the general government debt to gross domestic product at market prices is significantly below 60% and where risks in terms of long-term sustainability of public finances are low, the lower limit of the medium-term objective specified under point (b) can reach a structural deficit of at most 1.0% of the gross domestic product at market prices".

This means that the structural deficit must be equal to zero and that the cyclical deficit must be less than 3% of GDP, which is the maximum deficit allowed in the set of rules adopted by the European Union and known as the Stability and Growth Pact (SGP).

Contesting fiscal policy

The intellectual framework behind the TSCG is often labelled "neo-Keynesian" by experts. At the theoretical level, this framework clashes with the analysis proposed by RBCS. This school of thought asserts that economic agents react to fiscal policy outside of the automatic stabilisers in the form of an increase in the savings rate, which has the effect of negating the positive effects of fiscal measures.

In 1974, in the midst of the debate on the need for a fiscal stimulus policy in response to the oil crisis, Robert Barro, one of the first theorists of the real cycle, published a paper, "Are government bonds net wealth?" In this paper, the American economist proposed revisiting and providing a theoretical foundation for some of the representations of the 19th-century English economist David Ricardo on public finances. Regarding what went on to be called fiscal policy, Ricardo first argued that public debt is an artifice that allows the state to increase its spending without any immediate negative consequences for taxpayers.

He then wrote that "the amount raised by taxes to pay the interest of this loan, is merely transferred from those who pay it to those who receive it, from the contributor to the tax to the national creditor".[1]

Public debt thus underpins an underhand mechanism of income redistribution in favour of holders of government bonds and to the detriment of the population as a whole. Contrary to popular belief, it is not a transfer from one generation to another, but from one social class to another.

He then provides further insight:

"It is not then by the payment of the interest on the national debt that a country is distressed, nor is it by the exoneration from payment that it can be relieved. It is only by saving from income, and retrenching in expenditure, that the national capital can be increased; and neither the income would be increased, nor the expenditure diminished by the annihilation of the national debt. It is by the profuse expenditure of Government, and of individuals, and by loans, that a country is impoverished; every measure therefore which is calculated to promote public and private œconomy will relieve the public distress; but it is error and delusion, to suppose that a real national difficulty can be removed, by shifting it from the shoulders of one class of the community, who justly ought to bear it, to the shoulders of another class, who upon every principle of equity ought to bear no more than their share".[2]

[1] Ricardo, David (1816). *On the Principles of Political Economy, and Taxation*. London: John Murray, Albemarle-Street, p. 330.
[2] *Ibid.*, p. 336.

Robert Barro, referring to these writings, asserts that, anticipating a forthcoming tax increase in order to repay debt raised to finance the economic recovery, private economic agents accumulate financial assets that they will be able to liquidate to cope with the increased tax burden (hypothesis on the behaviour of economic agents, known as the rational expectations hypothesis). He states what economists have gone on to call the Ricardo–Barro theorem,[3] which is that public dissaving — that is to say, the budget deficit — generates an equivalent increase in private saving.

Put another way, any increase in public demand is matched by an equivalent decrease in private demand. Sticking to the Keynesian vocabulary, Barro writes that the multiplier is ultimately equal to [...] 0! This is known as the Ricardian equivalence, in reference to David Ricardo. The budgetary tool has been shaken, not to say discredited, and still the Queen of England's question goes unanswered.

What about monetary policy, which has been increasingly in the spotlight, especially since Irving Fisher highlighted the monetary aspects of the 1929 crisis?

Money and finance

The reason why monetary policy has become so important is that money has changed. For a long time, the money stock consisted of precious metals. At the beginning of the 19th century, David Ricardo considered that inflation was more of a geological phenomenon (the discovery of a new vein of gold) than an economic phenomenon. One of the characteristics of gold, apart from its relative rarity, is its weight. Small quantities of gold quickly become very heavy and therefore difficult to manipulate. The geographical expansion of trade was hindered by this characteristic, and so the world of commerce, independently of any act of state, sought to overcome this difficulty. This led to the use of promissory notes in long-distance trade. These notes could be exchanged for gold wherever there was a bank branch. While the state minted coins, the role of banks was to maintain a branch network accepting these coins in deposit and simultaneously putting into circulation banknotes convertible into gold, said to be "as good as gold".

---

[3]Also known as the Melon-Ricardo-Barro theorem, after Jean-François Melon [1675–1738], a French political economist.

Left to their own devices, banks quickly became convinced that it was absurd to leave the gold accumulating in their coffers idle. So, very pragmatically, they gradually put it back into circulation by lending it out.

Suppose a bank receives 100 in gold coins. It would then issue the equivalent in notes. Suppose then that, out of the 100 received in gold, the bank decides to lend 80. For reasons of convenience of use and ease of handling, which were already the reasons for the initial deposit, the borrower returns this gold to the bank in return for notes. The bank still has 100 gold coins in its coffers but has put the equivalent of 180 in notes into circulation. This is the beginning of "magical gold".

The bank repeats the process and lends some of the gold, say 64, which, according to the same pattern, is returned almost instantly. Thus, having accepted 100 in gold, the bank successively lends this gold to various borrowers, simply reducing each time the amount put back into circulation for prudential reasons. Each time, it lends γ times the amount it accepted (γ in Greek and c in Latin, the first letter of both credit and confidence in English), with γ being less than 1.

The total quantity of notes put into circulation by the bank will be

$$100 \times (1 + \gamma + \gamma^2 + \cdots + \gamma^n + \cdots)$$

The elementary mathematical result indicates that this algebraic expression is equal to $100/(1 - \gamma)$, which means that the quantity of notes put into circulation by the bank, also called fiat money, will tend towards

$$\text{Quantity of gold}/(1 - \gamma)$$

If the bank is not cautious, $\gamma = 1$, and the quantity of fiat money is potentially infinite. If it is very cautious, $\gamma = 0$, and the quantity of money in circulation is strictly equal to the initial quantity of gold. The emergence of a banking system gives rise to a fiat money creation process, which can be summarised as

$$\text{Deposit} \to \text{Credit} \to \text{Deposit}$$

The money supply created in this way is the sum of all the gold equivalents that banks have put into circulation and of all the commitments to supply gold that have been made by the banks. With all these commitments being recorded as liabilities, to calculate the money supply, one need only add up the banks' liabilities, net of their own funds. In this system, money creation is limited by two elements: the stock of gold and the calibration of γ, which governs the behaviour of banks and is based on so-called prudential rules. These rules can be based on the banks' own experience and wish to maintain an image of seriousness and rigour or be imposed by the public authorities. In theory, the quantity of money can nevertheless tend towards infinity: it is sufficient to relax prudential rules to the point where γ tends towards 1. In practice, as fiat money and scriptural money (i.e. current accounts that are substituted for notes) need to continue to be considered by the population as being "as good as gold", it is the prudence shown in this matter that ultimately determines the dynamics of money creation. If there is too glaring a mismatch between gold and "magical gold" in the money supply, the system runs the risk of facing what is known as a bank run, i.e. clients panic and rush to the bank to obtain the repayment in gold of the fiat and scriptural money they hold.

To thwart potential bank runs as much as possible, the authorities have not only tweaked prudential rules but also used many devices: putting obstacles in the way of gold convertibility, resorting to devaluations, i.e. reducing the physical quantity of gold to which one is entitled per monetary unit so as to increase the value of the gold stock, etc., until a simple but radical idea imposed itself: doing away with gold.

This came about in the 20th century, but it took two bites at the cherry. The first chapter was written on 21 September 1931, when the Bank of England suspended sterling's convertibility to gold.

When the then governor, Montagu Norman, took up his functions in 1920, he was blinded by his complete faith in the economic orthodoxy of the day and could not conceive the currency being anything other than gold or as good as gold. After the victory over Napoleon I, sterling's convertibility to gold was restored in 1819, four years after the end of the Napoleonic Wars. Sterling's convertibility to gold having been suspended during the First World War, Montagu Norman felt duty bound to restore convertibility in four years as before. To this end, he pursued a deflationary monetary policy, convincing, in the spring of 1925, the then Chancellor of the Exchequer, Winston Churchill, to return to the gold standard at the 1913 parity. Montagu Norman was certain he was in the right, even though the country's economic situation was deteriorating and he faced mounting criticism over sterling's overvaluation, notably from John Maynard Keynes. The 1929 crisis was a game changer. It amplified the country's trade deficit. Confidence was shaken, and the pound came under attack. Between January and July 1931, 20% of the

Bank of England's gold was withdrawn. On 21 September 1931, the government informed the Bank of England it would no longer defend sterling, which was left to float. In two months, sterling's rate of exchange against the US dollar fell from 4.86 to 3.25. Having followed proudly in the footsteps of Croesus and made gold the alpha and omega of money, Britain had been forced to take a step back.

At the Bretton Woods Conference in 1944, the United States formally restored gold's preeminent role in the international system. But that only lasted a while. First, on 15 August 1971, the United States President Richard Nixon announced the unilateral cancellation of the direct international convertibility of the US dollar to gold. But the second chapter really got under way on Monday 19 March 1973, when there was a chaotic reopening of foreign exchange markets, which had been closed since 1 March 1973. Devalued for the first time in December 1971, when the dollar price of gold was raised from $35 an ounce (set back in January 1934) to $38 an ounce, which was supposed to help reintroduce gold in the international system, the US dollar was devalued further on 12 February 1973. Would the new dollar price of gold at 42.20 an ounce hold this time? That was the question when markets reopened. The answer came in next to no time; traders massively sold their holdings of US dollars for gold or Deutsche marks. The obvious way to check this flight out of the US dollar would have been for the United States to raise interest rates so as to encourage banks to hold their cash there. The Nixon administration decided against this course of action, preferring to leave the dollar to the fluctuations of the market, leading to the adoption of the floating exchange rate system. The epilogue was written at the General Meeting of the International Monetary Fund held in Kingston, Jamaica, in January 1976. Further to the Jamaica Accords, changes were made to the articles of agreement that ratified two earlier decisions by the United States: on the one hand, the end of the convertibility of the US dollar into gold, decided by Richard Nixon on 15 August 1971; on the other hand, the introduction of floating exchange rates. This marked the end of Bretton Woods and, especially, gold's banishment from the monetary landscape.

The Jamaica Accords are a fundamental phase in the history of money because they mark a departure from the centuries-old use of money possessing, directly or indirectly, a physical form. This spectacular break with tradition did nevertheless leave a legacy, having laid the foundations for the practices of the modern banking system. Banks continue to create money through the credit mechanism, but without this being backed by an initial deposit, whether in gold or some other form of money. The money creation process, such as it is nowadays, has become

$$\text{Credit} \to \text{Deposit} \to \text{Credit}$$

In short, "loans create deposits". Economists the world over keep hammering home this point, notably during lectures when they pursue a career in academia.

In the financial statements published nowadays by banks, customer loans are recorded as assets and customer deposits (which can be expensed by customers at short notice) as liabilities. There follows that, to this day, the money supply (μ) is defined as the sum of the banks' liabilities, net of own funds and interbank loans, which is to say that money nowadays is not gold or some other commodity (for a long period and in large areas, American cigarettes served as a currency), but loans granted by banks.

While the banks' liabilities measure the money supply, assets comprise what are known as the money supply counterparts. The latter can be broken down into three large categories according to the borrowers' role in the economy: "Treasury", which records public debt held by the bank; "private investors"; and, finally, "foreign assets", which are assets denominated in a currency other than that of the bank's country of origin. These three categories correspond to the risk taken by the banks. Normally, loans to the Treasury are safe. Loans to private investors are secured on the assets of these investors, with the risk being that these assets might be overvalued. Foreign loans are supposed to be more uncertain and riskier. Note that a bank's assets also include loans to other banks (i.e. interbank loans), as well as the current account at the central bank. In short, money creation corresponds to an increase in the banks' liabilities, in accordance with the fundamental principle that loans create deposits.

Money creation arises from a bank's decision to grant a loan to fund the project of one of its clients, who may be from the private sector or from the public sector. Money creation arises from the activity carried out by commercial banks. Nowadays, money is created *ex nihilo*, based on the bank's analysis of the financial viability of the borrower's project. This is known as an "exchange of promises", the borrower committing, or, if you prefer, promising, to create the wealth needed to repay the loan principal and pay interest thereon.

Importantly, while bank lending has the consequence of increasing the money supply, a contraction in bank lending has the exact opposite effect.

Each time a bank's client repays part of a bank loan, it leads to a reduction in deposits and the quantity of money in circulation. In the 1930s, American economist Irving Fisher highlighted this mechanism as one of the causes that amplified the fallout of the 1929 crisis. Fisher explained to the Congressmen that "when you have [...] overindebtedness, and people try to get out of debt by liquidating [...] it causes distressed selling and the contraction of the currency, and therefore a fall in prices",[4] also a criminal wait-and-see attitude on the part of the government. That is the debt–deflation theory developed by Irving Fisher, the ravages of which John Maynard Keynes claimed could be remedied by substituting public debt for private debt so as to maintain the quantity of money in circulation.

However, before that, economists have mainly asked themselves how the banks' freedom to lend has turned the wheels of the economy, but by the same exposed it to an inflation risk. More concretely, the question is what limits bank lending? For the banks of old, lending was limited by the stock of gold and prudential rules. Is that still the case? On the face of it, nothing limits lending, except for the number of potential borrowers with profitable investment projects.

The greater freedom acquired in money creation along with the power given to banks have lent a new dimension to the notion of a crisis. Where crises in 19th-century writings were "commercial" or "industrial", they become "financial".

In 1998, commenting on the economic woes of certain Asian countries, first and foremost Thailand, Maurice Allais [1911–2010], winner of the 1988 Nobel Prize in Economic Sciences, highlighted this lack of limits and denounced its dangers and perverse effects, predicting that future crises would have a strong financial component. He wrote:

> "The 'miracles of credit' have been mentioned of old. For those in receipt of credit, there is indeed something miraculous about the credit mechanism, since it allows the creation ex nihilo of effective purchasing power that is exercised in the market, without this purchasing power being considered as remuneration for a service rendered.
>
> However, as much as the mobilisation of 'real savings' by banks to enable them to finance productive investments is fundamentally useful,

---

[4]Barber, William J. (1985).

the creation of 'false rights' through money creation is fundamentally harmful, both from the point of view of economic efficiency, which it compromises through the price distortions it creates, and from the point of view of income distribution, which is altered and made inequitable".[5]

If Maurice Allais did not pull his punches (employing terms such as "false rights" and "harmfulness"), he is not the only one to have expressed reservations about the "miracles of credit" and about this fundamental shift in paradigm, from "deposits create loans" to "loans make deposits".

In light of the ascendency of monetary policy, it is fashionable in Paris circles to follow, with some fascination, the decisions of the Federal Reserve System (the Fed for those in the know) and to marvel at its mandate, which is to conduct the nation's monetary policy to promote maximum employment and stable prices. The view is that this will ensure the United States enjoys harmonious growth, even as Europe remains in the throes of austerity, and will be shielded from any crisis.

But is this borne out? Not, perhaps, judging from Alan Greenspan's fate: the Fed chair was presented as a guru, a market whisperer, but then cast as the prime culprit for the 2008 bank debacle and 2009 recession. Cyclical downturns are now accompanied by tremors in the financial sector, which one would expect to be contained by the central bank. Yet, this has been the case only partially. When the Full Employment and Balanced Growth Act was passed in 1978, Paul Samuelson, who was awarded the 1970 Nobel Prize in Economic Sciences, had already questioned the compatibility of full employment and price stability (in light of the Phillips trade-off, later to become Mankiw's 10th Principle of Economics).

But one has to wonder whether the central bank is as powerful as people think or fear. Is it not a modern incarnation of the stagecoach fly in Jean de La Fontaine's fable? In "Stagecoach and the Fly", the stagecoach (the economy) drawn by six powerful horses (entrepreneurs) owes little to the fly (monetary policy), and for all of the fly's buzzing and stinging, the stage coach slows coming "up a steep hill and painful road of sand" and accelerates "upon the plain", the horses smoking and panting under the weight of the "women, old men and friars" (fiscal burden).

---

[5]Allais, Maurice (1993).

While monetary policy should not be neglected, it is important to understand its real power.

In reality, when it comes to the short term, the Federal Reserve's role is clearly defined in the act that was signed into law by President Jimmy Carter on 27 October 1978. However, it is not the incantations on full employment and price stability, the illusory nature of which Samuelson underlined, that really define its role, but its third goal, which is to promote moderate long-term interest rates. In the event of a cyclical slowdown, the increase in the cyclical public deficit provides the necessary support for activity. Low interest rates reduce the resulting interest burden. Fiscal policy has a memory: the public debt. Monetary policy is there to limit the consequences. In the long term, this goal is based on choices that are rarely mentioned today.

Foreign exchange policy in times of crisis

These policy choices are based on what economists call Mundell's impossible trinity, which deals with the relationship between capital flows, exchange rates and monetary policy. In terms of capital mobility, one can opt for total freedom of movement or impose capital controls. For interest rates, the choice is between an independent monetary policy and adopting the monetary policy of another country. For the exchange rate, the choice is between a stable exchange rate and one that is fluctuating, by allowing a floating exchange rate. According to Robert Mundell, the recipient of the 1999 Nobel Prize in Economic Sciences, the best combination would be the free movement of capital, an independent monetary policy and fixed exchange rates; however, all three objectives cannot be pursued simultaneously. As only two objectives can be pursued at a time, there are three possible policy combination options, i.e. monetary systems.

Since the 1844 Bank Charter Act, which regulated the issue of banknotes by the Bank of England and established the modern monetary system, all three monetary systems have been tested in turn. In 1844, Britain adopted the gold standard, combining fixed exchange rates with the free movement of capital. Any country adopting this policy combination *ipso facto* cannot pursue an independent monetary policy and is exposed to the same inflation as its trade partners. This system remained in place until January 1915. Accused, and rightly so, of being deflationary, it meant that a slowdown in the economic cycle was accompanied by a decrease in the general price level and wages. Crises experienced during this period often become social crises.

After 1918, in a report submitted in 1922 to the recently established League of Nations (the forerunner of the United Nations), Swedish economist Gustav Cassel [1866–1945] suggested maintaining fixed exchange rates, but introducing some flexibility by having adjustable exchange rates and then allowing each central bank to pursue an independent monetary policy. Mundell's impossible trinity meant that there was an end to the free movement of capital. Between 1922, when the Conference of Genoa adopted the recommendations of Gustav Cassel's report, and 1975, when the gold standard was abandoned at the General Meeting of the International Monetary Fund held in Jamaica, the monetary system was based on Mundell's second policy combination option, with fixed exchange rates and independent monetary policies, along with the widespread adoption of foreign exchange controls. Having announced the unilateral cancellation of the direct international convertibility of the US dollar to gold in 1971, it was the United States that, in 1976, ushered in the third policy combination option, namely an independent monetary policy and free movement of capital, *ipso facto* floating exchange rates.

Let's rapidly chronicle the rise and fall of each Mundell policy combination. The first was swept away by the First World War, not by its intrinsic weaknesses. The globalisation that got under way in the 1960s made it impossible to maintain the foreign exchange controls that were indispensable for the second policy combination. As for the third policy combination, which has survived to this day, its frailty is more glaring by the day. Far from leading to the balanced distribution of savings promised by its proponents, the monetary system is encouraging unbridled debt accumulation. Imbalances in current accounts on the balance of payments persist. In their answer to the questions asked by Queen Elizabeth II about the 2008–2009 recession, economists cited these imbalances as a major cause. The United States economy has run a current account deficit just about every year for half a century, accumulating a negative net international investment position (NIIP) representing almost 80% of GDP as of the end of 2021. Americans, the self-proclaimed "consumers of last resort" in the global economy, are living above their means without the floating exchange rate system correcting this situation by lowering the rate of exchange for their currency relative to other currencies. They have transformed their German, Japanese and, more recently, Chinese counterparts into the system's structural savers and now dream of seeing "the euthanasia of the rentier" come about. In the 1980s, the countries that went on to sign the Louvre Accord agreed to more or less exit the floating exchange rate system. Nothing came of it.

As you will have gathered, writing about crises is a real challenge. You cannot treat this subject without first acknowledging that any analysis cannot be exhaustive. However, never should the writer forget that one priority is to answer the questions of Queen Elizabeth II; one can therefore examine the phenomenon of crises by determining how historical reality fits with the more or less detailed presentation of the theories developed above. In practice, two types of crises can be identified: endogenous crises inherent to the functioning of the liberal market economy, which recur regularly and are therefore associated with the notion of a cycle; and exogenous crises, in which the economy suffers a shock that paralyses growth.

In the following chapters, we carefully examine how the endogenous crises of 1929, 1973–1975, 1992–1993 and 2008–2009 unfolded, as well as the exogenous crisis in 2020 triggered by COVID-19 and, finally, war-related crises.

Part II

A History of Crises

"Men only act in a state of necessity
and usually only recognise necessity
in a situation of crisis."

— Jean Monnet

Chapter 4

The Great Depression and Debt Deflation

The financial crises that strike the United States and the European Union generally unfold in two to three phases. During the first phase, when the financial crisis is triggered, the deterioration in the balance sheets of financial institutions, the fall in share prices and mounting uncertainty contribute to a contraction in lending, brought about by an exacerbation of adverse selection and moral hazard. This may lead to a second phase, characterised by a decline in economic activity, a banking panic and a malfunctioning of the credit channel. The combination of these factors can lead to a banking crisis.

If there is no resolution of the financial crisis, the economic downturn causes an unanticipated fall in the general price level, and the recovery process cannot kick in. A third phase then follows: debt deflation. When this happens, the unanticipated sharp fall in the general price level becomes entrenched, leading to a still greater fall in the net worths of businesses because of the increased debt burden. When debt deflation takes hold, problems to do with adverse selection and moral hazard are exacerbated, triggering a long-term depression in loans, investment spending and the overall level of economic activity.

For all those worried (or delighted, for there are some) by the difficulties of capitalist economies, the 1929 crisis is the mother of all crises, to be avoided (or at least meditated upon). The crisis had its genesis on 24 October 1929, with the fall in prices on the New York Stock Exchange. This day went down in the annals of history as Black Thursday. It was followed by Black Monday on 28 October and then Black Tuesday on 29 October. In one month, between mid-October and mid-November, the Dow Jones Industrial Average index lost 39% of its value, dropping from 326 to 198. The fall did not stop there, with the index hitting its all-time low on 8 July 1932, when it bottomed at 41.22.

This fall in share prices is just one of the many manifestations of the general collapse of Western economies. By 1932, 15 million Americans were unemployed, 10 times more than in the spring of 1929. Of course, everyone will have in mind Germany's dire situation, which swept Hitler to power on 30 January 1933.

Yet, when events started to unfold, for many economists, proceeding from an analysis of the business cycle, this was a simple correction. The New York Stock Exchange had surged by 120% between the start of 1926 and October 1929, and as conventional wisdom has it, "Trees don't grow to the sky". On 16 October, Irving Fisher, the most celebrated economist of the day, told members of the Purchasing Agents Association at its monthly dinner meeting that stock prices had reached "what looks like a permanently high plateau".

What Irving Fisher had in mind was that the surge in share prices had merely amplified the solid economic growth and resulting good corporate earnings. The 1920s were an era of prosperity, dubbed the Roaring Twenties by contemporaries. Between 1921 and 1929, American industrial production climbed by 50%. For France, the 1920s went down in the annals as the "Crazy Years",[1] when the ravages of the First World War (loss of an entire generation, wreck of agricultural land and industry) started to fade gradually.

Since then, historians have pored over hundreds of statistics and analysed in great minutia the sequence of events to explain how the world's economies went from boom to bust so suddenly. They singled out over-indebtedness, the passivity of central banks (which accepted and even provoked deflation) and the widespread adoption of protectionist measures (which stifled the dynamics of international trade and asphyxiated exporting economies, such as Germany).

One of the earliest reflections on the events of 1929 was shared by Joseph Alois Schumpeter [1883–1950] in a paper, "The present world depression: A tentative diagnosis," given to the Annual Meeting of the

---

[1] "Les Années Folles" in French.

American Economic Association held in December 1930. Referring to earlier comments about the choice of vocabulary, what will be noted is that this paper contains no reference to a crisis, but uses the term "depression". On the substance, the paper, similar to earlier texts, analyses the economic situation in the context of a cycle. For the first time, however, Schumpeter identifies three kinds of waves based on their length, what he calls the "long wave" or Kondratieff cycle determined by technological innovation, then what he says may be termed the Juglar cycle and, finally, the 40-month cycle. His view is that changes in production methods, in the broad sense of the term, in the post-war years created disturbances in the economy that led to the depression of the 1930s.

The "Great Contraction"

In their work, *A Monetary History of the United States, 1867–1960,*[2] Milton Friedman [1912–2006] and Anna Jacobson Schwartz [1915–2012] referred to the period from 1929 to 1933 as the "Great Contraction", explaining that it was by far the most severe business-cycle contraction in a century.

From the cyclical peak in August 1929 to the cyclical trough in March 1933, the stock of money fell by over a third, which more than halved money income (a 56% decrease) and contributed to a fall in prices of more than one third (a 36% decrease) over this near four-year period. Money income declined by 5% between 1929 and 1930, by 20% and 27% the next two years and then by a further 5% between 1932 and 1933. The rapid decline in prices meant that the declines in real income were relatively smaller, but even so, there were declines of 11%, 9%, 18% and 3% in the four successive years. The velocity of money (which tends to accelerate during the expansion phase of a cycle and to slow during the contraction phase) fell by nearly one third.[3] The suddenness of this fall underlines the severity of the contraction.

Over one fifth of the commercial banks in the United States, which held nearly one tenth of the volume of deposits at the beginning of the contraction, suspended operations because of financial difficulties.

---

[2]Friedman, Milton and Schwartz, Anna Jacobson (1963), p. 299.
[3]*Ibid.*, pp. 301–302.

Over this period, the number of commercial banks fell by well over one-third. Also, bank holidays were on a scale never seen before in the United States history, taking place in many states in early 1933 and nationwide from Monday 6 March to Monday 13 March 1933, involving not only all commercial banks but also the Federal Reserve Banks.

The bull market crashed in October 1929. Share prices peaked on 7 September 1929, with the Standard and Poor's composite price index of 90 common stocks reaching 254. On 29 October, this index fell to 162. This collapse negatively affected business sentiment. The uncertainty prompted consumers to consume less and entrepreneurs to invest less. By October 1930, production had fallen by 26%, prices by 14% and personal income by 16%. Between 1929 and 1930, the velocity of money slowed by 13%.[4]

As explained by Milton Friedman and Anna Jacobson Schwartz, a raft of bank failures in several states (particularly Missouri, Indiana, Illinois, Iowa, Arkansas and North Carolina) led to a contagion of fear among depositors, who rushed to convert deposits into currency as well as postal savings deposits. From $100 million in August 1929, postal savings deposits shot up to $1.1 billion in August 1929, underlining the spread of saver distrust towards banks.

The failure of 256 banks with $180 million in deposits in November 1930 was followed by the failure of a further 352 banks with over $370 million in deposits the following month. This included, on 11 December, the Bank of United States, which had over $200 million in deposits.[5] Besides this being a bank of systemic size, it was its distinctive name that gave the episode a particular global resonance. This turned into the first global financial crisis — the mother of all crises.

The surge in postal savings deposits is not the only measure of distrust in banks. With banks and investors searching for liquid investments, the change in interest rates also clearly shows the effects of the banking crisis. Government bond yields collapsed, whereas corporate bond yields soared. By reducing their portfolio of corporate bonds, banks amplified the crisis by heaping pressure on the bond market. With corporate bond issuance all but drying up, firms could not raise the long-term funds needed to invest.

---

[4] *Ibid.*, pp. 306–307.
[5] Annual Report of Superintendent of Banks, State of New York, Part 1, 31 December 1930, p. 46.

American investors withdrew funds from banks in Austria and Germany, two countries that became heavily indebted because of their obligation to pay war reparations following the First World War. In May 1931, Kreditanstalt, Austria's largest private bank, failed, which had repercussions across the continent and as far as the United States. This was followed by the closing of all banks in Germany on 14 and 15 July 1931 and the freezing of British short-term assets held by German banks. In July 1931, a one-year intergovernmental debt moratorium was instituted by President Hoover, along with a standstill agreement among commercial banks not to press for repayment of short-term international credits to provide temporary relief to the countries involved. These events led, on the one hand, to a repatriation of foreign investments (gold) in the United States. On the other hand, the United States commercial banks faced more problems, for they were left holding large amounts of short-term obligations of foreign banks, now frozen on balance sheets that already carried poor-quality real estate loans and were being undermined by the deflationary environment, all in the context of a global bank panic.

This flight of currency abroad was the economic and political *coup de grâce* for Austria and Germany, the two heavily indebted countries plagued by economic difficulties, with unprecedented inflation and unemployment. By impoverishing the population, this created a breeding ground for populism, paving Hitler's path to power.

In the United States, this gold inflow from abroad attenuated in the short term the downward pressure on the money stock caused by attempts by depositors to convert deposits into currency and by banks to add to their reserves in light of the deterioration in their liabilities. Despite the liquidity crisis facing the American banking system, there was no net change in Federal Reserve credit outstanding from February to mid-August 1931. The Federal Reserve did not inject additional liquidity, even though this could have greased the wheels of a banking system that was seizing up. What followed was a second acute banking crisis: in the six months from February to August 1931, commercial bank deposits fell by $2.7 billion, or nearly 7%, more than in the whole of the previous 18 months from August 1929 to February 1931.[6]

The financial turbulences led Britain to abandon the gold standard on 21 September 1931. Sterling weakened in the immediate aftermath of this decision, which triggered a global bank panic that engulfed central banks.

---

[6] *Ibid.*, p. 315.

Some 25 other countries followed Britain's lead. Because of the low level of money market rates in the United States and expectations that this country would also abandon the gold standard, the central banks of several countries (notably France, Belgium, Sweden, Switzerland and the Netherlands) converted substantial amounts of dollar-denominated assets in the New York money market to gold. These central banks also drew down deposits at the Federal Reserve in order to buy more gold, much of which was repatriated from the United States to these countries. Between 16 and 30 September, the United States gold stock fell by $275 million and then by a further $450 million in October. Bank failures jumped: 522 commercial banks with $471 million in deposits went under in October, followed by a further 875 banks with $564 million in deposits in the next three months. All in all, between August 1931 and January 1932, 1,860 banks suspended operations.[7]

Although the New York Federal Reserve did not act to ensure the liquidity of the internal market, it did step in to check the flight of capital abroad, raising its rediscount rate to 2.5% on 9 October, then to 3.5% on 16 October and continuing to raise the rediscount rate.

In response to the banking crisis, and at the recommendation of President Herbert Hoover, the Reconstruction Finance Corporation (RFC) was established by Congress in 1932 to make loans to banks and other financial institutions, as well as railroad companies, many of which were in danger of defaulting on their bonds. The corporation had an initial subscribed capital of $500 million. Over time, its borrowing capacity was increased from $1.5 billion to $3.3 billion. It was also authorised to advance up to $300 million to US states for unemployment relief.

The first Glass–Steagall Act[8] was passed on 27 February 1932. Initially, it was mainly designed to widen the circumstances under which commercial banks could borrow from the Reserve System and also to broaden the types of assets that could serve as collateral. One of the legislative sponsors, Carter Glass, a United States senator from Virginia, attempted unsuccessfully to pass other laws to regulate the activities of commercial banks.

---

[7] *Ibid.*, p. 317.

[8] The official title was "An Act to Improve the Facilities of the Federal Reserve System for the Service of Commerce, Industry, & Agriculture, to Provide Means for Meeting the Needs of Member Banks in Exceptional Circumstances, & for Other Purposes". Subsequently, more comprehensive measures were included in the Banking Act of 1933, enacted on 16 June 1933, which is now commonly known as the Glass–Steagall Act.

Under pressure from Congress, the Reserve System finally embarked on large-scale purchases of securities on the open market in April 1932. In four months, its security holdings jumped by roughly $1 billion.[9] However, the recovery spurred by this measure proved short-lived, being interrupted by another series of bank failures in the last three months of 1932. The reason was that, beginning in August 1932, the RFC started to publish the names of banks to which it had made loans in the preceding month. As clients interpreted the inclusion of their bank on this list as a sign of weakness, this triggered runs on individual banks, setting in motion a vicious circle that ultimately led to the banks' failure. As a result, even when banks needed to, they became reluctant to borrow from the RFC. Bank failures followed in quick succession. In response to the bank panics, statewide bank holidays were declared in many states.

These events elicited very much the same response from the Federal Reserve System as in September 1931. It raised discount rates in February 1933 to check the flight of capital abroad. After liquidity evaporated, it did not, however, attempt to counter the external or internal drain by embarking on massive open market purchases. At the start of March 1933, the New York Federal Reserve's reserve percentage fell below its legal limit. Governor Harrison asked Governor Meyer of the Federal Reserve Board to be allowed to run the bank with deficient reserves, and the board reluctantly agreed to suspend reserve requirements for 30 days.

In his first and memorable inaugural address on 4 March 1933, about one month after Hitler was named chancellor, Franklin D. Roosevelt asserted his firm belief that "the only thing we have to fear is fear itself".

A few days later, President Roosevelt proclaimed a nationwide bank holiday from 6 March until 9 March. A special session of Congress was called on 9 March, which enacted the Emergency Banking Act, confirming the powers of the president in proclaiming the bank holiday. The act dealt with unlicensed banks and authorised emergency issues of Federal Reserve Bank notes to meet currency needs.

Upon the passing of the Emergency Banking Act, President Roosevelt extended the bank holiday until 13, 14 or 15 March depending on the locations of the banks. Only banks licensed by the federal or state banking authorities were allowed to reopen. The president also suspended the payment of notes in gold as well as exports of gold.

---

[9]Friedman, Milton and Schwartz, Anna Jacobson (1963), p. 322.

The regulations devised and enacted by the United States government at that time prevented other crises like the one in 1929 from occurring. The governments that followed gradually dismantled these regulations until the Clinton administration undid what was left of them and allowed the same circumstances as in 1929 to resurface, leading to the crisis of 2008.

Chapter 5

The 1975 Recession

In the final volume of his memoirs, Henry Kissinger explained that "Until 1972 the United States had been in a position to control the world price of oil because it was producing well below full capacity. Thus America was, in effect, able to set the price by increasing or withholding production".[1] At the start of the year, the Texas Railroad Commission, the organisation establishing ceilings on American production, authorised full production in reaction to the very high level of demand. This decision ended the United States' ability to set the world oil price. At the same time, at the start of the 1970s, the governments of oil-producing countries nationalised oil-production operations. Created in 1960, the Organization of the Petroleum Exporting Countries (OPEC)[2] took over the role of the Texas Railroad Commission after 1972. OPEC's mission is to ensure the stabilisation of oil production and prices through the allocation of production quotas to each of its members. In 1972, crude oil prices jumped 40%, but they did so from a very low base and at a time when "industrial democracies" were enjoying a period of prosperity. As a result, although this price increase marked not just a change in the economic environment but a change of epoch, it passed largely unnoticed.

---

[1] Kissinger, Henry (2020), p. 665.
[2] Founded by five countries: Iran, Iraq, Kuwait, Saudi Arabia, and Venezuela. It currently has 13 members: Algeria, Angola, Congo, Equatorial Guinea, Gabon, Iran, Iraq, Kuwait, Libya, Nigeria, Saudi Arabia, United Arab Emirates, and Venezuela.

Kissinger, in his memoirs, writes:

"It was the Middle East War of 1973 that gave oil-producing countries the pretext for unleashing their new bargaining power to its full extent. On October 16, 1973, OPEC raised the price of oil by 70%, from $3.01 a barrel to $5.12. On October 17, the Arab OPEC oil ministers met in Kuwait and agreed to reduce OPEC production by 5% in order to sustain the higher oil price. On October 18, Saudi Arabia, as a sign of solidarity with the Arab cause, cut its production by 10%. On October 20, to protest the American airlift to Israel, Saudi Arabia announced a total embargo of oil exports to the United States and also to the Netherlands, which was deemed too supportive of Israel".[3]

In reality, the surge in oil prices was not the consequence of the embargo or even the production cutbacks, as Venezuela, Nigeria and Iran made up for the shortfall in Saudi Arabian deliveries, but caused by the wind of panic that swept across the so-called "industrial democracies". The latter rushed to build up inventories to levels far exceeding their needs, exacerbating the shortages they wanted to avoid.

This was amplified by the fact that, on 22 and 23 December 1973, in Teheran, two months after the end of the Middle East War, the Gulf members of OPEC more than doubled the price of oil again, to $11.65 a barrel, meaning that this price jumped 387% in two months.

The surge in oil prices was studied closely by other commodity-exporting countries that thought they could do as OPEC and raise prices for their production.

In the speech given before the Ninth World Energy Conference in Detroit, President Gerald Ford stated: "Sovereign nations cannot allow their policies to be dictated or their fate decided by artificial rigging and distortion of world commodity markets. No one can foresee the extent of damage, nor the end of the disastrous consequences if nations refuse to share nature's gifts for the benefits of mankind".[4]

Very early on, Henry Kissinger pleaded for a concerted answer by industrial democracies to OPEC countries. His view was that "the energy problem is soluble only on a cooperative basis. The stakes go beyond oil

---

[3] Kissinger, Henry (2020), p. 666.
[4] *Ibid.*, pp. 678–679.

prices and economics and involve the whole framework of future political relations. If producers continue to manipulate prices and consumers fail to develop an effective response, a major power shift is inevitable. The producers will be able to shake the world banking system by virtue of their ability to manipulate their assets. Oil revenues will become the source of ever-spiraling arms races threatening the world peace. Western unity will disintegrate if the industrial democracies do not regain both the sense and the actuality that they control their destinies".[5]

In response to the oil shock, "industrial democracies" put up a united front, culminating in the Rambouillet Summit, which was labelled a summit of the principal economic powers. French President Valéry Giscard d'Estaing, as the host, extended formal invitations to the United States, Britain, Germany and Japan. Gerald Ford pushed for the inclusion of Italy and Canada. Reluctantly, the French President agreed to Italy's attendance, but not to Canada's.

During the summit, Giscard d'Estaing lamented that "we have not had more coordination in our energy program. [...] We must, therefore, limit the amount of money we spend on oil imports and decide what steps could be taken to avoid further balance of payments problems resulting from new oil price increases".[6]

The economic turning point

In 1974, the oil price shock led to an additional annual trade deficit of $125 billion in 1997 dollars for the countries of the Organisation for Economic Cooperation and Development (OECD).[7] The economic repercussions were even more severe for the non-oil-producing countries of the developing world.

The energy crisis broke when the era of floating exchange rates was just getting under way. The switch to a system of floating exchange rates took place in three stages. The first occurred on 15 August 1971, when President Richard Nixon announced that he had directed Treasury Secretary Connally to suspend the convertibility of the dollar into gold and to close the gold window used by foreign central banks to exchange dollars for

---

[5] *Ibid.*, p. 681.

[6] *Ibid.*, p. 695.

[7] *Ibid.*, p. 664.

gold. This severed the link between the dollar and gold. The second occurred in December 1971 with the Smithsonian Agreement, with the monetary authorities of the world's leading developed countries agreeing to modify exchange rates, marking the demise of the gold standard. The final chapter was written on 19 March 1973 when, after an exceptional closure in response to an intense bout of speculation surrounding the US dollar, the foreign exchange market reopened and most currencies were left to float against the US dollar. No longer having to defend their currencies under this new floating exchange rate system, a number of countries adopted expansionary policies in the 1970s, which contributed to driving up inflation.

As summed up rather cynically by John Bowden Connally (who served as Treasury Secretary during Richard Nixon's presidency) when he addressed a French delegation, "the dollar is our currency, but it's your problem". It was to address this "problem" that, in 1979, the European Community established the European Monetary System, a multilateral adjustable (but nearly fixed) exchange rate system, paving the way for the adoption of the single currency in 1999. In this way, a new currency area was born!

While in Paris on a state visit, Richard Nixon presented French President Georges Pompidou with a fragment of lunar rock brought back by the Apollo 11 mission. Keen to impress his American counterpart, the French President gifted a thorn retrieved from the Crown of Thorns relic, to the astonishment of the Catholic Church, which had not been informed. Since its purchase from a Venetian merchant by Louis IX (commonly known as Saint Louis) in 1239, the relic has been the property of the French State and the Catholic Church. Over the centuries, the Crown of Thorns has been used to seal alliances. With the benefit of hindsight, one could say that since Nixon was instrumental in the creation of the euro, the thorn he was gifted was just reward, though it is not known whether President Pompidou managed to impress his guest.

The oil shock marked a turning point for unemployment and real GDP growth in the industrialised world. Whereas between 1963 and 1972 the unemployment rate reached 4.7% in the United States, 1.9% in Europe and 1.2% in Japan, it jumped to 7%, 5.5% and 1.9%, respectively, between 1973 and 1982. Unemployment continued to rise inexorably after that, with the unemployment rate in Europe reaching 9.4% between 1983 and 2006, 7.8% between 2007 and 2009 and then 10.1% between 2010 and 2015.

Between 1961 and 1972, GDP growth averaged 4.2% in the United States, 5.1% in Western Europe and 9.5% in Japan. Growth pulled back to 2.9%, 2.8% and 4%, respectively, between 1973 and 1981.

At the start of the 1970s, even before the oil shocks, inflation was already a widespread problem. Between 1963 and 1972, it reached 3.3% in the United States, 4.4% in Europe and 5.6% in Japan. It jumped to 8.7%, 10.7% and 8.6%, respectively, between 1973 and 1982. The quadrupling of oil prices between 1973 and 1974 constituted an exogenous shock since it was of OPEC's doing, applying very significant inflationary pressure. The rise in the general price level was driven by the indexation of wages to prices; mechanisms of this type had been implemented by most industrialised countries at the end of the 1960s to protect purchasing power against inflation. The rise in oil prices prompted speculators to hoard other commodities to play a rise in their prices, which, when it happened, drove up inflation. As explained by Paul Krugman, "Over the following years, central bankers proved unwilling to combat these inflationary pressures at the cost of yet-higher unemployment".[8]

Normally, inflation tends to accelerate during the expansion phase of a cycle and slow down during the contraction phase. Yet, between 1974 and 1975, even as GDP contracted, output stagnated and unemployment increased; inflation in fact accelerated. To describe these unusual conditions, economists coined a new term: stagflation.

As explained by Paul Krugman:

"Stagflation was the result of two factors:
(1) Increases in commodity prices that directly raised inflation while at the same time depressing aggregate demand and supply.
(2) Expectations of future inflation that fed into wages and other prices in spite of recession and rising unemployment."[9]

---

[8] Krugman, Paul, Obstfeld, Maurice and Melitz, Marc (2009).
[9] *Ibid.*, pp. 541–542.

According to the report produced by Paul McCracken,[10] by careful management and the limitation of short-term growth ambitions, it should be possible to achieve both satisfactory expansion and steady disinflation. In a similar vein, the OECD Economic Outlook No. 22[11] noted that "further expansionary policy action would be necessary while avoiding a very sharp pick-up of activity and an associated acceleration of inflation".[12]

The OECD Economic Outlook No. 22[13] also argued that "countries in strong balance-of-payments positions should take up slack faster than countries in a weak position. This view was contested by a number of countries, typically those identified as 'best placed' to expand, such as West Germany and Japan. Questions were also raised about whether it was possible to secure durable expansion through fiscal policy; whether there was a stable, long-term trade-off between inflation and unemployment; whether disinflation could be achieved without monetary rigour; whether income policies were realistic except in very specific periods and (smaller) countries; and whether the public sector should seek to reduce the share of national resources it absorbed".[14]

At the 1978 G7 Summit in Bonn, "West Germany and Japan agreed to adopt fiscal stimulus measures in exchange for a commitment from the United States to raise its domestic oil price to world levels and the European commitment to reach a successful conclusion of the multilateral trade negotiations within the General Agreement on Tariffs and Trade (GATT)".[15]

A new paradigm is "a new way of perceiving and analysing the subject of study".[16] In their report, *OECD at 50: Evolving Paradigms*, the authors concluded the following:

"A prominent paradigm shift took place in the early 1980s when policies became more oriented towards the medium term and the supply

---

[10]McCracken, Paul (1977).
[11]OECD (1977).
[12]OECD (2011).
[13]OECD (1977).
[14]OECD (2011).
[15]*Ibid.*
[16]*Ibid.*

side took centre stage in response to the stagflation of the 1970s. Since then there have been further developments in the paradigm, such as those associated with the rational expectations revolution which called for predictability and transparency of policymaking. The 'Great Moderation' of stable growth and prices since the mid-1990s was seen as evidence of the paradigm's success. However, favourable headline statistics masked growing underlying imbalances, and when these erupted with the financial crisis of 2008–09, established certainties again broke down and new approaches to policymaking came to the fore".[17]

Western countries and oil

The 1973 oil shock triggered a crisis that, according to Henry Kissinger, lasted a decade. The energy crisis subsides for periods of time, only to spring back with greater force, unannounced. It has lurked behind all the fiscal and financial crises experienced since then. The Yellow Vests crisis in France, which broke out on 17 October 2018, was initially a protest against an expected rise in fuel prices, notably diesel, after the government announced plans to jack up the domestic consumption tax on petroleum products (taxe intérieure de consommation sur les produits énergétiques, TICPE). It is a good illustration of how the energy crisis has kept rearing its head. Climate disruptions, which are increasingly manifest in everyday life, mean that energy crisis brings with it more acute hazards. There needs to be a structural response through innovations such as green hydrogen. Climate disruptions and the end of cheap oil make an ecological revolution vital. The energy crisis brings us back to the simple reality that there are more and more of us on Earth with access to limited and rapidly diminishing fossil energy sources. Despite the sophistication of our societies, our primary needs have not changed (food, shelter, etc.) and have been the root cause of all crises since the dawn of time.

The United States had not said its last word in 1972. With the recession of 1975 came the realisation that the country's energy dependence was its Achilles' heel. In 2018, the country's gas production increased dramatically, saturating the domestic market. That year, the United States

---

[17]*Ibid.*

accounted for 21.5% of natural gas production in the world. Russia was the second-largest producer with 16.3%, followed by Iran with 6.2%, Canada with 4.8% and Qatar with 4.5%.[18]

Over the past 10 years, shale gas exploitation has changed the geo-economic world order, with the United States seeking to exploit the advantage procured by this new energy source, particularly in its trade exchanges with Europe. Russia's war with Ukraine has seen the United States expand its end markets for gas at prices significantly higher than those commanded by Russian gas. This forced change of gas supplier is likely to fuel inflation in the European Union.

The challenge for modern society remains energy, which is finite, when energy consumption keeps on increasing. Added to this is the fact that, to this day, oil and gas supplies depend on the most politically unpredictable regions of the world. A repeat of the 1974 oil shock is therefore more likely than not. The European Union's dependence on Russian gas demonstrated the limits of our economic model in the face of Russia's invasion of Ukraine. The Fukushima-Daiichi nuclear accident in 2011, the fraught situation of Ukrainian nuclear power plants located in a war zone, the dependence on high-risk countries for the uranium needed for the operation of nuclear power plants and the risk of nuclear proliferation would suggest that nuclear energy is not necessarily a long-term alternative.

Franz Kafka's short story, *A Little Fable*, illustrates our response to the energy crisis and climate disruption:

> ""Alas", said the mouse, "the whole world is growing smaller every day. At the beginning it was so big that I was afraid, I kept running and running, and I was glad when I saw walls far away to the right and left, but these long walls have narrowed so quickly that I am in the last chamber already, and there in the corner stands the trap that I must run into".
>
> "You only need to change your direction", said the cat, and ate it up".[19]

---

[18] https://www.ege.fr/infoguerre/gaz-de-schiste-aux-etatsunis-enjeux-strategiques-et-politiques.

[19] East of the Web, http://www.eastoftheweb.com/cgi-bin/version_printable.pl?story_id=LittFabl.shtml.

All that was needed was indeed a change of direction. Will the COVID-19 pandemic and Russia's war on Ukraine be enough to convince us to change course? Will it merely lead to Russian gas being displaced by American shale gas, which would neither resolve the climate crisis, nor open the way to an ecological transition on the scale of the Industrial Revolution?

Chapter 6

1993 Crisis: OECD Employment Strategy

To a large extent, the 1993 recession was typically cyclical. In France, for example, the downturn set in as early as 1991. It was particularly pronounced in the United States, pointing to a recession in 1992. Observing the slowdown in growth, James Carville — an adviser to Bill Clinton, the Democratic presidential candidate, who was trailing far behind incumbent George Bush in the polls ahead of the November 1992 elections — confidently told campaign workers to focus on one slogan: "It's the economy, stupid". He was convinced that the cyclical downturn would be the undoing of George Bush, and he was right.

Cyclical downturn: Fiscal policy to the rescue

At the start of the 1990s, leading economies experienced a contraction in activity, which was staggered over time. It started in the United States, before spreading to Britain, then Continental Europe and Japan. The American economy contracted by 0.7% in 1991, the British economy by 0.6% in 1992, the German economy by 1.2% in 1993, the French economy by 0.6% in 1993 and, finally, the Japanese economy by 0.5% in 1993.

If this crisis was cyclical in nature, the indicator that should be examined is the output gap. This is the difference between actual GDP and potential GDP. When an economy produces more than its potential level of output, the output gap is positive, but as the economy is working over-time, this comes at the cost of creating inflationary pressures.

When the output gap is negative, the economy is producing less than it should, which leads to unemployment. Statistics at the turn of the 1990s indicate that the output gap swung from positive to negative, leading to an increase in unemployment. In practice, the output gap is the difference between actual GDP and potential GDP expressed as a percentage of potential GDP.

In the United States, the output gap was −1.3% in 1990 and −1.7% in 1991, which helped Clinton win the presidential election. In Germany, the output gap swung into negative territory in 1993, deteriorating from +1.4% in 1992 to −1.3% in 1993. This was also the case in France, with the output gap deteriorating from +1.1% in 1992 to −1.4% in 1993. The downturn started to take hold in 1991, with the cycle trough being reached in 1993, which is when the crisis took its toll. France was in an unfavour-able situation when this downturn occurred, having failed to restore its fiscal situation during the boom phase of the cycle. It headed into reces-sion with a hefty structural deficit (3.8% in 1990). In reality, the govern-ment, which still struggled to reason in terms of cycles, did not really grasp that a cyclical downturn was taking hold.

In January 1993, at a time when some economic institutes were already predicting there would be a recession, France's Prime Minister was still forecasting growth of 1.2%. Yet, indicators pointing to a worsen-ing situation were multiplying, particularly in terms of the budget's execu-tion. The initial 1992 Finance Act put the deficit at 90 billion francs. The Amending Finance Act at the end of the year put the deficit at 184 billion francs. It came out at 226 billion francs. This had two consequences: (1) the primary fiscal balance, which had been positive before interest payments, turned negative to the tune of 52 billion francs; (2) with a defi-cit of 3.2% in 1992, France found itself in breach of commitments given to the European Union just months before.

France signed the Maastricht Treaty on 7 February 1992, the treaty being ratified in September 1992 following a referendum. The treaty lim-ited the government deficit to 3% of GDP. France had a deficit of 6% in 1993. The analysis of this deficit between its structural and cyclical com-ponents put the structural deficit at 4.7% of GDP. This was not only due to fiscal insouciance, no doubt, but also a desire to compensate for a very restrictive monetary policy pursued to address the turbulences in the for-eign exchange market.

European specificity: EMS crisis

Revisiting the origins of the crisis in a paper published by Observatoire français des conjonctures économiques (OFCE) in April 1994, French economist Pierre-Alain Muet arrived at the following diagnostic:

> "The successive recessions experienced by industrialised countries at the start of the 1990s combined to varying degrees three factors responsible for slowdowns:
>
> — The downturn of the investment cycle following the boom enjoyed in the second half of the 1980s;
> — The bursting of financial and real estate bubbles; and
> — A tightening of monetary policies in reaction to the acceleration of inflation".[1]

This diagnosis contains the key elements explaining a crisis: the cycle as modelled by the Hansen–Samuelson oscillator model, in which investment plays a major role; more or less speculative mechanisms associated with uncontrolled credit expansion; and misguided economic policies, in this case maintaining an excessively restrictive monetary policy.

This last factor concerned more particularly Europe. In the same paper, Pierre-Alain Muet concluded that the "1992–1993 recession shows Europe suffering fundamentally from its inability to pursue coordinated and coherent policies in the face of cyclical adversities".[2]

These European approximations were reflected in the European Monetary System (EMS) crisis of September 1992. This foreign exchange crisis was triggered when the Danes said "no" to the Maastricht Treaty in the referendum held in June 1992. At the end of August, uncertainty over the outcome of the referendum in France on the same subject led many observers to predict an uncertain, if not unlikely, future for European monetary integration.

These doubts were heightened by events in Germany. On 30 June 1990, the government decided to introduce the Deutsche mark as the official currency of East Germany in preparation for its reunification with

---

[1] Muet, Pierre-Alain (April 1994).
[2] *Ibid.*

West Germany. East German marks were exchanged for Deutsche marks on a 1:1 basis, but applying a less favourable exchange rate above certain limits and depending on personal conditions (age, country of residence). The Bundesbank was up in arms over this measure, arguing that it would considerably weaken the competitiveness of the East German economy, which, as it was becoming apparent, was in dire straits. The central bank made the case that, before the fall of the Berlin Wall, the Deutsche mark was worth 20 Ostmark. Helmut Kohl argued that the currency exchange, in that it amounted to setting an exchange rate, was a decision for the government, outside the Bundesbank's purview. The Chancellor also put forward eminently political reasons for the government's decision. Admittedly, the 1:1 exchange rate was generous, but as the Chancellor pointed out, one of the slogans taken up by East German protesters was that "if the Deutsche mark comes we will stay; if it doesn't come we will go to it!",[3] which would have emptied East Germany of its population. Monetary unification was followed shortly after by political reunification on 3 October. In its wake, Germany rediscovered something it thought it had left behind: inflation. In 1992, post-reunification, average inflation culminated at 5.2% when it reached 2.4% in France. The Bundesbank responded by raising interest rates.

Under the EMS, there were fixed exchange rates between the currencies of most countries belonging to the European Economic Community and the Deutsche mark. With capital controls having been lifted, Mundell's impossible trinity required these countries to pursue the same monetary policy as the Bundesbank. France, Italy, Spain (which joined the EMS on 19 June 1989) and the United Kingdom (which joined the EMS on 6 October 1990) were forced to tighten their monetary policy. This is what is referred to as a "procyclical" measure, i.e. one that tends to increase the effects of the cycle, in this case the slowdown in growth, when economic policy is intended to be "countercyclical". Some market operators considered that this theoretical aberration could not last. In their view, the EMS, undermined technically by Germany's monetary policy and politically by the Danish "no", was doomed. These operators engaged in systematic speculation, at the risk of causing an implosion of the system, which led to a sharp appreciation of the Deutsche mark. This type of speculation is based on a quite simple

---

[3] Sen, Ashish Kumar (2021).

principle. Speculators borrow francs, liras, pesetas or pounds that are immediately converted into marks. The German currency is provided by Banque de France, Banca d'Italia, Banco de España and Bank of England, drawing down on their currency reserves until these are exhausted. These central banks then borrow marks from the Bundesbank, which has an infinite supply of marks since it prints the country's money. As for the mechanics, let's say that the speculator borrows 100 francs that are converted into marks. If there is no devaluation, when the loan is repaid, the speculator still has 100 francs but must repay this principal plus interest and will therefore be out of pocket. The speculator will be in pocket if, in the interval, there has been a devaluation of the franc against the mark to an extent such that this covers the cost of the loan. Quite simply, speculation will fail if there is no devaluation, i.e. by ensuring that each Deutsche mark demanded in the market is supplied. This will be the case if the Bundesbank decides to create more marks, placing them on the market either directly or indirectly by lending them to other central banks, in our example to the Banque de France.

Aware of this reality, authorities managing fixed-rate exchange rates implemented rules to ensure speculation failed. The simplest rule is for the central bank of the country attracting speculative capital to accept to create as much money as needed to absorb the demand. That was provided for under the Bretton Woods system, which called for devaluations to be decided in concert, not under the pressure of speculation. In the case of the EMS, this rule was adopted in September 1987 at the meeting of economics and finance ministers held in Nyborg, Denmark, which then held the presidency of the European Economic Community. The rule adopted at this meeting is that the central bank under attack raises its interest rates (i.e. use of interest rate differentials) to make the price of borrowing by speculators as prohibitive as possible. Concurrently, the central bank with the diverging currency (i.e. attracting speculative capital) creates as much money as needed.[4]

---

[4]With the rules endorsed by economics and finance ministers at the summit held in Nyborg, the intention was to address speculation relying exclusively on monetary policy measures. At a conference held at Princeton University back in 1972, when the US dollar was the object of intense speculation, James Tobin proposed completing the monetary response by adding a fiscal element in the form of a tax. His proposal was to apply a tax to each short-term currency trade (in our example the purchase of marks with francs) to

On 11 September 1992, the till-then simmering speculation intensified. The Italian lira was first in the firing line. The Nyborg rules came into play: Banca d'Italia raised its rates, while the Bundesbank flooded the market with 24 billion Deutsche marks. Very soon, however, the Italian government concluded that a devaluation would not have only negative effects, notably in that higher inflation would make it easier to pay back government bonds. Banca d'Italia decided to call it a day, and the lira was devalued by around 7% in the EMS. This was the first change of parity since 1987, since Europe, in the spirit of the Louvre Accord and with the creation of the EMS, committed to a real and lasting fixed exchange rate system.

On 16 September, it was sterling's turn to be in the firing line. In London, John Major's government was not at all in the same frame of mind as Giuliano Amato's government in Rome. It baulked at the very idea of a devaluation. The Bank of England raised its interest rates and waited for the Bundesbank to supply the Deutsche marks needed to defend the exchange rate between the British and German currencies. It waited in vain.

The most spectacular outcome of the September 1992 crisis was sterling's forced exit from the EMS. In refusing to support the Bank of England, the Bundesbank booted Britain out of Europe. John Major had kept at bay British Eurosceptics, first as Chancellor of the Exchequer under Margaret Thatcher (ousted for her increasingly anti-EU views) and then as Prime Minister. On 16 September 1992, John Major found out that, while British Eurosceptics had the merit of being brazen in their opposition, he had fallen foul of more devious adversaries in French and German "Anglosceptics".

When the market opened on 17 September, it was the franc that came under attack. After Italy and Britain threw in the towel, Franco-German solidarity was put to the test. In contrast with what happened with sterling, France and Germany played by the Nyborg rules. Banque de France raised its rates, which reached 13% on 23 September, while the Bundesbank lent the marks needed to fend off speculation. By 4 p.m. on 23 September, sales of French francs had ceased and speculators had capitulated: the

---

hurt and thus deter speculators. The Tobin tax was born! The American economist would later deplore that his idea was misappropriated and turned into a slogan. It is true that his work and ideas deserve better than the partisan half-truths of which he was the victim.

ESM was saved, with it the project for an Economic and Monetary Union. Admittedly, this project did not emerge totally unscathed from these turbulences.

As if to draw a line under the events of the autumn of 1992, in an interview he gave that summer, before the EMS crisis and on the eve of the Danish referendum expected to return a "no", Milton Friedman [1912–2006], the famous winner of the 1976 Nobel Prize for Economic Sciences, was asked about his thoughts on Europe's plan for one currency, to which he replied: "I believe it will not come to an achievement in my lifetime".[5]

One of the fallouts of what must be termed a "foreign exchange crisis" is that interest rates were at record highs for some time. At the end of 1992, short rates, at three months in France, still towered at 10% even though inflation was only 3%. A situation that prompted some to salute Britain's wisdom (short rates in London pulled back to 6.8%, with the real rate, after deducting inflation, at less than 4%) and denounce Germany's egoism, even as a recession, spurred by an ultra-restrictive monetary policy and the evolution of the cycle, looked to be on the cards in 1993.

OECD draws lessons from the crisis

Nearly two decades after the 1977 McCracken Report, which was supposed to draw practical inferences from the 1975 recession, the OECD embarked on the drafting of a new report that looked into the challenges raised by the 1992–1993 crisis. In 20 years, inflation is no longer the central issue it was when the McCracken report was published, having been replaced by unemployment. In 1993, the unemployment rate reached 10.1% in France and 7.8% in Germany. Back in 1989, which was the most favourable year in the cycle, it reached 7.9% in France before the crisis pushed up unemployment. The unemployment rate rose high in France, which was far from being an isolated case. This led the OECD to publish a report on this issue in 1996, *The OECD Jobs Study*, which has since been reassessed at regular intervals.

---

[5]Interview with Milton Friedman, 1 June 1992, https://www.minneapolisfed.org/article/1992/interview-with-milton-friedman.

Key policy recommendations are grouped under 10 headings:

(1) Set macroeconomic policy such that it will both encourage growth and, in conjunction with good structural policies, make it sustainable, i.e. non-inflationary.
(2) Enhance the creation and diffusion of technological know-how by improving frameworks for its development.
(3) Increase the flexibility of working-time (both short-term and lifetime) voluntarily sought by workers and employers.
(4) Nurture an entrepreneurial climate by eliminating impediments to, and restrictions on, the creation and expansion of enterprises.
(5) Make wage and labour costs more flexible by removing restrictions that prevent wages from reflecting local conditions and individual skill levels, in particular for younger workers.
(6) Reform employment security provisions that inhibit the expansion of employment in the private sector.
(7) Strengthen the emphasis on active labour market policies and reinforce their effectiveness.
(8) Improve labour force skills and competences through wide-ranging changes in education and training systems.
(9) Reform unemployment and related benefit systems — and their interactions with the tax system — such that societies' fundamental equity goals are achieved in ways that impinge far less on the efficient functioning of labour markets.
(10) Enhance product market competition so as to reduce monopolistic tendencies and weaken insider–outsider mechanisms while also contributing to a more innovative and dynamic economy.[6]

What is being advocated is clear: flexibility, competition, training adapted to the reality of the labour market, development of entrepreneurial spirit. The recommendations have the merit of going beyond a simple combination of lower charges and the social treatment of unemployment.

The first recommendation, despite its brevity, is the most immediate response to the challenges posed by a crisis. It clearly affirms the idea that a crisis is inherently cyclical. This harks back to the idea of a

---

[6]OECD (2006).

"temporary downturn" in production to be addressed through short-term economic management, while long-term problems affecting potential growth and structural unemployment find their solution in the next nine recommendations. The challenge for short-term economic management is that it needs to be "countercyclical", that is to say, it should be conducted such that it will limit the scale of the crisis. What is implicitly criticised by the OECD in the first recommendation of its Jobs Strategy are "procyclical" policies, that is to say, policies that, far from improving the situation, in fact aggravate the crisis. The monetary policy conducted by Europe in 1992 was dictated by foreign exchange considerations, with a manifest political element. From the strict standpoint of economics, however, the obvious defect of this monetary policy was that it was procyclical.

The OECD theorises the medium-term impact of the crisis and economic policy response using the so-called recovery alphabet, distinguishing between U-, V- and W-shaped recoveries. A U-shaped recession exit signifies a protracted recovery, V-shaped a faster recovery, and W-shaped a recovery dashed by another downturn. After the 1993 crisis, Japan experienced a U-shaped recovery, some observers describing it as an L-shaped recovery, in reference to the pedestrian pace and weakness of this recovery. After the 2009 crisis, the Euro area's recovery was W-shaped. After the 1953 recession, the United States experienced a V-shaped recovery, leading to full employment.

Three conclusions can be drawn in support of a V-shaped recovery, which remains the best option:

(1) One must accept the idea that the recovery depends essentially on the responsiveness of businesses. The strength and vigour of the recovery are directly linked to the extent to which the productive fabric emerges unscathed from the crisis. If the number of failures/bankruptcies increases during the crisis, the rebound capacity is that much less. To preserve the productive fabric, the tax burden needs to be lightened during the downturn, while taking advantage of the upturn to restore public finances. This equates to pursuing a fiscal policy based exclusively on automatic stabilisers.

(2) One needs to abandon old-fashioned stimulus packages based on increased public spending, even when justified by the benefits of investment or by the agreed political discourse about "spending for

the future". Fiscal policy needs to be based on automatic stabilisers and should not get lost in phantasmagorical stimulus packages of the kind seen in 1975. Recoveries that rely on a stimulus of this kind increase the debt and trigger Ricardian equivalence mechanisms, consistent with the economic theory developed by Robert Barro, with no tangible result other than the need for a correction. As a result, the austerity plans that follow these stimulus packages lead to a W-shaped recovery.

(3) It is vital to devise a better response to alternating oil shocks and countershocks, and their impact on the purchasing power to achieve greater consumption stability.

Chapter 7

2008 Crisis and Quantitative Easing

Pauperisation of Americans and subprime mortgages

It is the manner of the state's intervention in the economy as well as its economic objectives that determine the people's prosperity. As explained by American economist Richard Musgrave [1910–2007] in his book, *The Theory of Public Finance*,[1] published in 1959, the state fulfils three economic functions: the allocation function, the distribution function and the stabilisation function.

In his book published in 1986, Hyman Minsky considered that "economic policy[2] must reflect an ideological vision; it must be inspired by the ideals of a good society. And it is evident that we are faced with a failure of vision, with a crisis in the aims and objectives that economic policy should serve".[3]

In 1926, John Maynard Keynes defined the political problem as a need "to combine three things: economic efficiency, social justice, and individual liberty. The first needs criticism, precaution, and technical knowledge; the second, an unselfish and enthusiastic spirit that loves the ordinary man; the third, tolerance, breadth, appreciation of the

---

[1] Musgrave, Richard (1959).
[2] Regarding the origins of the term economy and other economic terms, see Leshem, Dotan (2016).
[3] Minsky, Hyman P. (1986).

excellencies of variety and independence, which prefers, above everything, to give unhindered opportunity to the exceptional and to the aspiring".[4]

For Keynes, the "distribution of wealth" has a proven macroeconomic utility as it contributes to supporting consumption, the main component of aggregate demand. His view is that there is no opposition between economic efficiency and taxation, an assertion successfully demonstrated by Nordic countries:

> "The outstanding faults of the economic society in which we live are its failure to provide for full employment and its arbitrary and inequitable distribution of wealth and incomes. [...] Moreover, experience suggests that in existing conditions saving by institutions and through sinking funds is more than adequate, and that measures for the redistribution of incomes in a way likely to raise the propensity to consume may prove positively favourable to the growth of capital".[5]

Keynes concluded that "in contemporary conditions the growth of wealth, so far from being dependent on the abstinence of the rich, as is commonly supposed, is more likely to be impeded by it. One of the chief social justifications of great inequality of wealth is, therefore, removed".[6]

Apart from the humanist aspect, Keynes believes in the economic efficiency of the "welfare state" that developed after the Second World War. Aggregate wealth that is better distributed increases aggregate demand and thus contributes to economic growth. Furthermore, this helps reduce the political risk, as populism prospers in inegalitarian societies. This is what might be called "socialist Keynesianism".

While Ronald Reagan is considered the "liberal" par excellence, "the market, which was seen as a problem from the 1920s to the 1970s, became a solution under Reagan".[7] As he stated in a message to Congress:

> "My program — a careful combination of reducing incentive-stifling taxes, slowing the growth of Federal spending and regulations, and a

---

[4]Keynes, John Maynard (1972).
[5]Keynes, John Maynard (1936), Chapter 24.
[6]*Ibid.*
[7]Daniel, Jean-Marc (2021), pp. 301–302.

gradually slowing expansion of the money supply — seeks to create a new environment in which the strengths of America can be put to work for the benefit of us all".[8]

He is, in reality, a right-wing Keynesian, which came at a huge cost for the American people:

"The programme is clear and implies a disengagement of the State. What is striking, however, is that nowhere in this programme [...] is there any mention of the fiscal deficit. Compared with the Kennedy years or what went on under Labour in the United Kingdom, this is less a revision than a mutation. The intention is not to resolve the deficit, but to generate it differently. No more spending on social programmes to reduce poverty. Economic recovery no longer involves expanding public demand but steadily expanding private demand, through repeated tax cuts. Right-wing Keynesianism continues to base economic growth on short-term support for demand, but does so by cutting taxes".[9]

After the "Glorious Thirty", with the energy crisis and tax cuts for the most well-off taxpayers, "it is the beginning of the end"[10] for the prosperity of Western society. From that point on, to maintain their standard of living, Westerners have lived on credit, while states have taken on more and more debt, leading to an increasingly higher individual debt spread over increasingly longer periods.

In an American society where the poor were becoming poorer and poorer, subprime customers dreamt of owning their home, just like in the films they saw on television. That is the American dream. The banks lent their customers the money they needed to buy their principal residence at adjustable rates with very high margins and then securitised these subprime loans, i.e. high-risk mortgages, in order to sell them on as

---

[8] Reagan, Ronald (1982).
[9] Daniel, Jean-Marc (2021).
[10] "C'est le commencement de la fin", Charles-Maurice de Talleyrand-Périgord on news of Napoleon's retreat from Moscow and the battle and crossing of the Berezina River in the winter of 1812.

investments, allowing the banks to externalise the risk while earning high returns.

The subprime crisis could not have started in France because French banks do not lend on the basis of the property's value, arranging a mortgage as collateral, but on the basis of the borrower's income. As a result, French subprime customers cannot become homeowners. In 2017, 62% of French households in the lowest 20% income band were tenants,[11] bearing in mind that renting ultimately comes at a far greater cost than home ownership.

Affordable housing should be available to all citizens in the world's leading economies. Yet, this is not the case. Concentrations of wealth (or poverty) create speculative bubbles that eventually burst, shaking the entire economy. Such is the degree of interaction and integration at the global level that the repercussions are felt across the world. The bill for this concentration of wealth is footed once more by the poorest, whether they are Americans, Europeans or from other parts of the world. Keep in mind that the stimulus packages were designed to help the banks out of the mess they got the economy into, not to help their subprime customers. No grace period, debt restructuring/reorganisation or concessional rates were provided for subprime customers to help them meet loan repayments. Customers were left facing the very real prospect of losing the fruits of a lifetime, forced into selling their home at a price that did not even cover the outstanding loan, for when the subprime bubble burst, the property market crashed under the weight of forced sales.

Louis-Ferdinand Céline published two novels around the time of the 1933 crisis, which bore much resemblance to the 2008 crisis and in which everything is said about the market economy. *Voyage au bout de la nuit* (1932)[12] describes the efforts of a young Frenchman to make his fortune in the United States, in the colonies, and whose attempts also fail in France because he is not part of the establishment. It would seem that the New York and Paris of the 21st century have not changed much. His second novel, *Mort à crédit* (1936),[13] tells the story of a Frenchman's efforts to repay the loan he took out to buy his main residence. Repaying the loan becomes his life's sole endeavour, his *raison d'être*, to the point where,

[11] https://www.insee.fr/fr/statistiques/4764315.
[12] *Journey to the End of the Night* (1932).
[13] *Death on Credit* (1936). aka *Death on the Installment Plan* for the American edition.

having scrimped and saved, he doesn't see that the house is going to rack and ruin. He sacrifices everything to pay the loan instalments, even his morning paper. When he does pay the final instalment, he's lost, having nothing to live for.

The Great Recession

While the genesis of the crisis can be traced to the United States high-risk mortgages, i.e. subprimes, it affected all industrialised economies and in particular those of the European Union. The 1929 crisis, which also had as its origin United States mortgage lending, was also more devastating for Europe than for the United States.

When the 2008 crisis erupted, adverse selection[14] and moral hazard in the credit markets were intensified by uncertainty created by the failure of a large number of financial institutions across the world, the deterioration in the balance sheets of credit institutions holding subprime loans, liquidity problems at undercapitalised banks and the more than 40% fall of stock markets.

The recession that got under way in December 2007 led to the most severe economic contraction since the Second World War. For this reason, it was termed the Great Recession in the United States. Yet, the contraction in economic activity was far less than during the Great Depression of 1929, as both governments and central banks intervened massively to restore confidence, maintain liquidity in the interbank market and support commercial banks so that they might continue to finance the economy. The government implemented programmes to save distressed financial institutions and industries, notably the automotive industry. Nevertheless, the crisis did lead to a historic slump in global trade, a slowdown in global economic growth and an exponential rise in unemployment. The European Union took much longer to recover from the crisis than the United States. The only crumb of comfort was that deflation was avoided thanks to the responsiveness of the European Central Bank (ECB) and Federal Reserve and their unconventional monetary policies, notably quantitative easing. We discuss the actions of central banks later in this chapter.

---

[14]Adverse selection refers to a situation in which the buyer is less well informed than the seller about the quality of the asset. Because of this asymmetric information, also called information failure, the buyer is at risk of overpaying for the asset.

World trade between all countries and for nearly all goods collapsed by 20% between 2008 and 2009. Global exports fell by more than 15% between December 2008 and March 2009. Three factors have generally been responsible for slumps of this magnitude: protectionism, consumer behaviour and credit crunch.

In contrast to the 1930 slump, when protectionism was the response to the financial crisis, which caused economies to plunge, trade barriers were not erected during the 2008 crisis.

Consumer behaviour changes during times of crisis. There is a shift away from top-of-the-line products towards lower-cost items, contributing to a reduction in the value of world trade. In addition, consumers and businesses tend to put off investment spending. Purchases of capital goods, which accounted for 20% of world exports and 25% of France's exports, were deferred, the crisis having eroded confidence and led to a decline in income. This explains, in part, the slump in world trade.

The credit crunch contributed to the spectacular slump in world trade. To export, businesses will often take out loans or credits, given the extended lead times until delivery, as well as to fund expenditures incurred to enter and maintain a presence in foreign markets. They also need to take out cover, in the form of letters of credit, documentary credits or international guarantees, against the financial risk associated with international transactions. Funding and insurance are typically provided by commercial banks under trade finance facilities. Trade is governed by rules established by the World Trade Organization (WTO). The credit crunch affected mainly small- and medium-sized enterprises that, having limited cash resources, found it increasingly hard to self-finance their exports and therefore maintain a presence in export markets.

During the Great Recession, Germany put in place an aid plan for its banks; however, as the government demanded the suspension of the variable element of the remuneration of bank executives and of dividend payments for the duration of the bailout, few banks were encouraged to sign up to the plan.

In contrast to France, which decided to support the country's banks so that they might continue to finance the economy and thus "preserve the economy in its essentials", the German government extended direct financing to competitive medium-sized enterprises, which had demonstrated exceptional potential internationally, lest these businesses should lose ground at the global level. In the wake of the subprime crisis, the German government placed these measures at the core of its stimulus strategy, which proved a winner in terms of the trade balance and employment.

One of the ways in which these measures were put in place was via the programmes of the KfW Bankengruppe, one of the top 10 banks in Germany, which has a less concentrated banking sector than France. KfW[15] had been founded 60 years before, in 1948, as part of the Marshall Plan for the reconstruction of the German economy. The banking group is owned 80% by the Federal Republic of Germany and 20% by the federal states, i.e. the Länder. Its mandate is to improve economic, social and environmental living conditions in Germany, Europe and across the globe. For example, one of the group's entities, KfW Mittelstandsbank,[16] provides long-term loans at preferential conditions to small- and medium-sized enterprises, business founders, start-ups and self-employed professionals. The group stimulates innovation and the capital risk market, advances environmental protections and supports the development of communal infrastructures. Besides financing investments in Germany, KfW extends export and project finance, fosters cooperation with developing countries and provides a range of advisory and other services.

As a rule, medium- and intermediate-sized enterprises have more difficulty accessing credit than large enterprises, particularly during a crisis. Also, interest rates will be less competitive than those negotiated by large enterprises. During the subprime crisis, KfW contributed to the functioning of the credit channel by making available to enterprises a credit envelope of €15 billion in 2008 and then a further envelope of €100 billion in 2009. The loan limit for financing working capital was €50 million for a small- or medium-sized enterprise, with loans for a period of at most eight years. Loans were granted at competitive rates. This gave German small- and medium-sized enterprises a real head start in the global race, at a time when their French counterparts were at a handicap on the international stage.

G20 asserts itself

As indicated above, the first summit of the Group of Six (G6) was hosted by Valéry Giscard d'Estaing in Rambouillet in response to the 1973

---

[15]Kreditanstalt für Wiederaufbau, or Credit Institute for Reconstruction.
[16]Literally KfW SME.

energy crisis. This unofficial forum brought together the heads of the richest industrialised countries in the world: France, the United States, Britain, Italy, Japan and Germany. As revealed by Henry Kissinger in his memoirs, as surprising as it may appear, it was not the agenda that created frictions but which countries to invite to the summit. That Valéry Giscard d'Estaing should bar Canada from this summit, despite perhaps half of the population being French speakers, remains incomprehensible to this day.

> "It turned out that what caused the greatest controversy was not the agenda, on which agreement was reached fairly quickly, but the composition of the conference. [...] Ford, supported by Wilson, argued on behalf of including Italy and — more passionately — Canada. Finally, Giscard, who as the host was by diplomatic protocol entitled to extend the formal invitations, agreed on Italy's attendance.
>
> Giscard remained adamantly opposed to the inclusion of Canada, however. [...] Ford was irate because he thought Giscard was abusing the technical advantage of being the host and because Canada was our principal trading partner. At first he considered refusing to attend the summit but eventually relented, though not without vowing to behave coldly towards Giscard — a threat that did not survive the first half-hour of the next private meeting between the two Presidents".[17]

Canada joined the G6 in 1976. Russia joined what was then the G7 in 1998.

The G20 was created on the sidelines of the G7 meeting held in Washington on 25 September 1999 at the initiative of Canada's Finance Minister, Paul Martin, and in response to the financial crises experienced by emerging countries in the late 1990s. The G20 can be defined as an intergovernmental forum intended to promote international economic cooperation and address major issues with a long-term vision. The G20 is composed of the world's 19 largest economies and the European Union. Its members account for 80% of world GDP, 75% of world trade and 60% of the world population. It was the financial crisis of 2008 that put the G20 centre stage, relegating to the backstage the G7 and G8, no longer

---

[17] Kissinger, Henry (2020), pp. 692–693.

considered representative enough to address global financial crises, given the place occupied by emerging countries. The G20 summits were initially ministerial-level meetings attended by finance ministers and central bank governors. At the initiative of French President Nicolas Sarkozy, the meeting on 15 November 2008 was the first attended by heads of state and government.

Russia's war on Ukraine set back global cooperation at the G7 level because, when the conflict broke out, China and India did not condemn the Russian invasion, giving them a competitive advantage, since they were able to buy oil and gas from Russia at a quarter of the price. Cheaper energy and the weakening of Europe as a result of the war have accelerated global dynamics, propelling China to the top and allowing India to quickstep into China's former role as the "world's factory". When the ones to benefit from the surge in oil and gas prices caused by the West's response to the war on Ukraine should have been just commodity-exporting countries (such as Algeria, Angola, Chile, Colombia, Ghana, Kazakhstan, Nigeria, Qatar, Saudi Arabia, and the United Arab Emirates), several major importers (including China and India) have also shared in the spoils.

Although everyone analyses economic policy into "procyclical" and "countercyclical" measures, every brutal downturn in growth prompts apocalyptic comments, as if the cycle did not exist and recessions were unpredictable. The reaction of governments is to explain that, while difficulties arise from the "irrational exuberance of the markets", the return to growth will be the fruit of their regulatory wisdom. To lend credibility to this assertion, world leaders gather at summits, which are solemn and elaborate affairs, seen by some as the economic "high mass" of the international calendar.

In November 2008, the United States was the host nation. The presidential transition was under way, with President George W. Bush serving out his second term of office, while his successor, Barack Obama, had just been elected. Neither gave the impression of being hugely concerned about the economic difficulties that were brewing. As a result, it was the Europeans who set the stage. As France held the presidency of the European Union, this G20 meeting has gone down as the high point in Nicolas Sarkozy's political career. The embellished story of these times casts him as the saviour of the world economy, working, in his words, at a "re-foundation of capitalism". In fact, it was rather HM Treasury that was at the helm. It quietly convinced world leaders to back a plan based on supporting the banking sector, going so far as to nationalise certain banks, and implementing a quite conventional package of fiscal measures to support an economy on the back foot. In 2007, relative to GDP, fiscal deficits reached 2.8% in the United States, 0.7% in the euro area, 2.7% in the United Kingdom and 2.4% in Japan. By 2009, fiscal deficits had deteriorated to 11.2% in the United States, 6.4% in the euro area, 11.4% in the United Kingdom and 8.7% in Japan.

Commenting on the implementation of these stimulus plans, Dominique Strauss-Kahn, who was attending the G20 summit in his capacity as the managing director of the International Monetary Fund (IMF), declared during the closing press conference that nearly all the participants had backed the IMF's proposal to use the fiscal tool and placed the emphasis on a coordinated fiscal stimulus in order to be more effective, concluding that as a result, the situation was really changing. The 2008–2009 crisis marked the start of an unprecedented escalation in both public and private debt.

By 2016, when one can consider that the 2008–2009 crisis was over, the world's debt stood at $164,000 billion, or 225% of GDP. It consisted of 63% private debt and 37% public sector debt.

Just as after the 1975 crisis the OECD published "Towards full employment and price stability — A report to the OECD by a group of independent experts"[18] and then after the 1993 crisis *The OECD Jobs Study*, in 2009 it published the "OECD strategic response to the financial and economic crisis — Contributions to the global effort", aimed at "tackling regulatory and policy failures comprehensively", with "the focus [...] on the interactions between finance, competition and governance, and, ultimately, on achieving sustainable growth".

It summarised its recommendations as follows:

"In the current context, an optimal policy strategy to restore sustainable long-term growth should include the following key components:
- keeping markets open;
- sound macroeconomic, fiscal and labour market policies for stability and resilience;

---

[18]Commonly known as the McCraken Report.

- fostering a 'green' and innovation-led recovery;
- advancing development; and
- balancing markets and policies and fostering exit from public ownership".[19]

It was an ambitious programme for sure!

As for the International Monetary Fund, in its *2010 Annual Report*, it explained that the 2008 crisis started in "advanced" countries and spread rapidly to the rest of the world:

> "The global financial crisis that erupted in 2008 took a devastating toll on the world economy. The availability of credit fell, trade collapsed, capital flows dried up, growth slumped, and unemployment rose significantly. While the epicenter of the crisis was a number of advanced economies (and specifically the financial sectors in those countries), the crisis was quickly transmitted to all corners of the globe".[20]

Thanks to global cooperation, marshalled by France, the global financial system did not collapse, but growth in developed countries was permanently reduced and with it the standard of living in those countries:

> "Policymakers responded to the crisis by implementing a set of bold and aggressive monetary, fiscal, and financial sector policy measures that were delivered in an environment of unprecedented cooperation. These concerted policy actions were successful in arresting and then reversing the downward economic spiral. Financial market conditions improved, and the first signs of an emerging recovery became evident in the second half of 2009 with growth gaining steam in early 2010. Nevertheless, the recovery remained moderate and uneven, with advanced country growth relatively weak, but emerging markets and low-income countries generally rebounding strongly".[21]

---

[19] OECD (2009).

[20] International Monetary Fund (2010).

[21] *Ibid.*

The action of central banks

The central banks' mandate is to ensure the stability of the economy. To this end, banks seek to control short-term interest rates in the central bank money market by regulating supply through operations conducted under market conditions, thereby ensuring the liquidity of financial markets.

Conventional monetary instruments employed by central banks fall into three categories: reserve requirements, standing facilities and money market operations proper, also known as open market operations.

Given the magnitude of the 2008 crisis, the ECB and Federal Reserve were forced to take exceptional measures, referred to as unconventional monetary policy operations, to stabilise the economy in a context where monetary policy transmission was not working because of the malfunctioning of certain market compartments. The situation was such that even if the central banks had lowered rates, this reduction would not have been transmitted to the entire economy. Because of the unaccustomed mistrust between banks and the fact that they did not know which among them held subprime products and what the valuation of these products might be, the interbank market had seized up, leaving it more than ever to central banks to manage liquidity to prevent a collapse of the global financial system.

The unconventional monetary policy instruments involved:

- the supply of liquidity, through facilitated access to the discount window, temporary funding facilities (such as the Term Auction Facility, TAF), emergency loans and easing of collateral rules, with these measures being intended to avoid the collapse in the prices of most asset prices;
- asset purchase programmes to complete the supply of liquidity, with direct purchases of securities, which would otherwise drag in their fall all other securities, thereby limiting contagion and restoring confidence.

In November 2008, the Federal Reserve announced large-scale purchases of fixed-rate, mortgage-backed securities (MBSs) guaranteed by Fannie Mae, Freddie Mac and Ginnie Mae. In total, $1,250 billion of agency MBS were purchased. Quantitative easing 1 (QE1) was the term coined to refer to these large-scale purchases. In November 2010, it was followed by quantitative easing 2 (QE2); the Federal Reserve announced that it would purchase $600 billion of long-term Treasury securities, with the intention of lowering long-term interest rates. On 12 September 2012, the Federal Reserve announced that it would begin purchasing agency MBS at a pace of about $40 billion a month to support the property market in particular and the financial markets in general until unemployment subsided.

Quantitative easing, which refers to the aforementioned programmes, led to a dramatic increase in both the Federal Reserve's balance sheet and the money supply. The Federal Reserve's balance sheet was approximately $800 billion in September 2007. As a result of the management of the subprime crisis, it reached $3,276 billion on 24 April 2013.[22]

The expression "quantitative easing" has been attributed to Richard A. Werner. When working in Tokyo in 1994, he coined the expression during a presentation to Japanese investors. It then appeared in a newspaper article, "How to create a recovery through 'Quantitative Monetary Easing'".[23] that he published in the Nihon Keizai Shinbun (Nikkei) in September 1995. The German economist explains the causes of banking crises and proposes monetary policies to resolve these crises and stimulate a swift recovery. In this article, this new concept of monetary policy is applied theoretically to the Japanese situation. As it turned out, Japan was in fact the first country to apply quantitative easing in 2001 in an attempt to extricate itself from a deflationary monetary situation dating back to 1997.

To counter a deflationary risk, the central bank will carry out large-scale and prolonged purchases of long-term debt securities. The consequence is a decline in long-term interest rates and money creation that act on the real economy through the four monetary policy transmission channels, namely:

- *Interest rate channel*: the offer of financing at low interest rates by commercial banks and financial markets facilitates access to credit for households, businesses and the state, which has the consequence of driving up consumption and investment;

---

[22] Mishkin, Frederic S. (2013).
[23] Werner, Richard A. (2 September 1995).

- *Expectations channel*: with quantitative easing, households, businesses and the state anticipate interest rates will remain low, encouraging them to consume and invest, in turn boosting household demand and business investment;
- *Asset price channel*: financial asset portfolios of economic agents are reallocated, with the rise in the price of certain assets leading to a wealth effect for their owners, enabling them to consume and invest more;
- *Exchange rate channel*: quantitative easing has the consequence of weakening the currency of the country or monetary area, which favours exports and increases import prices.

Following the global financial crisis, to get the credit channel to function, many central banks embarked on quantitative easing beginning in 2008. Support plans for commercial banks during the subprime crisis had as objective to improve the banks' access to liquidity and facilitate their short- and medium-term refinancing by creating additional liquidity channels. The goal was to limit the transmission of the financial crisis to the real economy through the credit channel. This is because, according to the theory of the credit channel *stricto sensu*, as developed by Ben S. Bernanke and Alan S. Blinder,[24] under the assumption of imperfect substitutability between bank loans and other financial assets, i.e. on the asset side for banks and on the liability side for borrowers, following an exogenous monetary policy shock, such as a rise in the cost of interbank loans and advances, banks will adjust asset portfolios and scale back lending, while non-financial agents will reduce investment or consumption spending.

Two months after the collapse of Lehman Brothers, the Federal Reserve implemented its first quantitative easing programme in November 2008.

The Bank of England resorted to quantitative easing for the first time in 2009.

In July 2012, to restore confidence in the markets, Mario Draghi stated that "Within our mandate, the ECB is ready to do whatever it takes to preserve the euro. And believe me, it will be enough".[25] Shortly after,

---

[24]Bernanke Ben S. and Blinder, Alan S. (1988).
[25]https://www.youtube.com/watch?v=W97hM8eCE5g.

the ECB went on to announce a new programme of open-ended, unlimited buying of government bonds, what it termed "outright monetary transactions", but it was never activated as Mario Draghi's intervention had instantly restored confidence.

The ECB announced an expanded asset purchase programme on 22 January 2015.[26] The central bank added the purchase of sovereign bonds to its existing private sector asset purchase programmes in order to address the risks of too prolonged a period of low inflation and thus contribute to a return of inflation rates towards 2%. Under this programme, "combined monthly purchases will amount to €60 billion. They are intended to be carried out until at least September 2016. [...] The ECB will buy bonds issued by euro area central governments, agencies and European institutions in the secondary market against central bank money, which the institutions that sold the securities can use to buy other assets and extend credit to the real economy. In both cases, this contributes to an easing of financial conditions".[27]

Not taking into account the ECB's Pandemic Emergency Purchase Programme (PEPP), the Eurosystem purchased €3,169 billion under its quantitative easing policy.

The effects of quantitative easing are felt over the medium term, as the stock of sovereign and corporate bonds held by the ECB would guarantee low rates for 10 years even if the institution stopped these purchases, which was not on the agenda then.

In 2021, the ECB explained that "asset purchases, also known as quantitative easing or QE, are one of the tools that we at the ECB use to support economic growth across the euro area and bring inflation to our 2% target".[28] It will not have escaped you that the unconventional tool has become conventional, or as the playwright Eugène Ionesco wrote in *Exit the King*, "Now it's so normal to be abnormal, there's no such thing as abnormality. So that's straightened that out".[29]

The question is whether, by accelerating money creation, quantitative easing really does stimulate the real economy and generate inflation over the medium term. The answer is: it all depends on how this money

---

[26] https://www.ecb.europa.eu/press/pr/date/2015/html/pr150122_1.en.html.

[27] *Ibid.*

[28] https://www.ecb.europa.eu/ecb/educational/explainers/show-me/html/app_infographic.en.html.

[29] Ionesco, Eugène (1963).

creation is used. If money creation adds to the banks' reserves and the target federal funds rate is near its lower bound of zero, the benefits of quantitative easing will be slow to come. In Japan, the first country to resort to quantitative easing, not only was there no economic recovery, but the general price level declined. For this reason, Ben Bernanke preferred the expression "credit easing" over "quantitative easing" when referring to the measures taken by the Federal Reserve. By modifying the balance sheet structure, these measures enabled certain segments of the credit market to function without necessarily triggering an economic recovery.

Researchers at the Federal Reserve Bank of New York concluded, in 2010, that the quantitative easing during the subprime crisis led to reductions in longer-term interest rates on a range of securities, including securities that were not included in the purchase programmes.[30] Their view is that these reductions in interest rates primarily reflected lower risk premiums rather than lower expectations of future short-term interest rates.

Would Irving Fisher have wanted central banks to go to such lengths in 2008 to avoid deflation?

Had the Federal Reserve rescued the Bank of United States and Lehman Brothers, the crises of 1929 and 2008 might have been nipped in the bud. Central banks and regulators did allow the conditions necessary for a financial crisis to resurface, but the immediate aftermath of the 2008 crisis was more ably managed than that of 1929. As recommended by Irving Fisher in 1933, central banks injected enough liquidity in 2008 to sever the link between deflation and over-indebtedness and extricate the economy from a vicious deflationary circle.

What was not done during the Great Depression was done during the Great Recession. The 2008 crisis should really be called the 2007 crisis, as it broke out on 9 August 2007 when BNP Paribas announced it was suspending the calculation of net asset value as well as transactions for three of its funds exposed to the subprime market because of the impossibility to value certain assets. The global scale of the crisis became

---

[30] Gagnon, Joseph *et al.* (2010).

apparent as soon as it flared, as the flash point was a French bank, when the problem stemmed from asset-backed securities relating to high-risk mortgage loans distributed on a grand scale by American banks. However, it was Lehman Brothers Holdings Inc. seeking Chapter 11 protection on 15 September 2008 that marked the collective consciousness, and what should have been known as the 2007 crisis went down in the annals as the 2008 crisis. This was a systemically important bank, and its collapse sent tremors through the global financial system, much as did the closure of the Bank of United States on 11 December 1930. Yet, the 1929 crisis did not change its name to the 1930 crisis!

Having allowed history to repeat itself, it was to the central banks' credit that they had learned the lessons from the 1929 crisis and did manage the subprime crisis more ably.

Commercial banks fund themselves by borrowing short-term on the interbank market. The start of the subprime crisis was characterised by banks' mistrust of each other because of uncertainty over each bank's exposure to subprime mortgages. The fact that banks were reluctant to lend money to each other disrupted the functioning of the interbank market, leading to a significant rise in three-month rates. Normally, the spread between the three-month interbank rate and the central bank's key rate did not exceed 20 basis points. From August 2007, this spread doubled, and at times, it was up to six times wider.

To reduce tensions in the interbank market, ensure bank liquidity and thus restore confidence, central banks injected massive amounts of liquidity, as Irving Fisher had recommended in 1933. The ECB was the first to inject an amount corresponding to the interbank market's liquidity needs in a single operation. This measure is all the more commendable given that the ECB was, at the time, a very young central bank, having been created on 1 June 2008, when the Federal Reserve System was established on 23 December 1913. The Federal Reserve, on the other hand, had more difficulty calibrating this need, so it took several injections to address liquidity needs:

- As early as 9 August 2007, when BNP Paribas suspended transactions for three of its funds with exposure to the subprime market, being unable to determine a fair value, the ECB conducted a fine-tuning operation with same-day settlement and overnight maturity, injecting just under €95 billion of liquidity in the overnight money market.

- On 9 August 2007, the Federal Reserve injected $24 billion, a further $38 billion on 10 August, $38 billion on 27 September and, finally, $41 billion on 1 November.

As can be seen, the total amount injected by the Federal Reserve was more or less equivalent to the ECB's first injection, which led to Ben Bernanke being accused, and rightly so, of not doing enough to provide liquidity.

- On 12 December 2007, the Bank of Canada, Bank of England, European Central Bank, Federal Reserve and Swiss National Bank announced concerted measures, including temporary reciprocal current arrangements (swap lines), to provide dollars to address the elevated pressures in short-term funding markets. The Federal Reserve established a TAF to provide funds to depository institutions; the first auction was for $20 billion, which was then gradually increased, reaching $100 billion in March 2008.
- On 18 December 2007, the ECB injected over €348 billion through an exceptional two-week main refinancing operation (MRO), having announced that this would be conducted on a full allotment basis. In 2008, the maturity of these operations was extended to six months.

In response to the crisis of confidence triggered by Fannie Mae and Freddie Mac being placed into conservatorship on 7 September 2008 and then the collapse of Lehman Brothers on 15 September 2008, concerted measures were announced by some of the world's leading central banks on 18 September 2008, creating reciprocal swap lines or expanding existing ones for a total amount of $180 billion:

- This was followed up by an announcement on 13 October 2008 by several leading central banks that they would conduct tenders of US dollars for full allotment.
- On 29 October 2008, the Federal Reserve, Banco Central do Brasil, Banco de Mexico, Bank of Korea and Monetary Authority of Singapore announced the establishment of temporary reciprocal swap lines.

- On 25 November 2008, the Federal Reserve announced the creation of a $200 billion facility to support the issuance of asset-backed securities (ABS) collateralised by student loans, auto loans, credit card loans and loans guaranteed by the Small Business Administration.

The Federal Reserve also announced that it would initiate a $600 billion programme to purchase the direct obligations of housing-related government-sponsored enterprises (GSEs) and MBSs backed by these:

- On 18 March 2009, the Federal Reserve announced plans to purchase up to $300 billion of longer-term Treasury securities and raised ceilings for the purchases of agency MBSs and agency debt.
- On 6 April 2009, the Federal Open Market Committee authorised new temporary reciprocal swap lines with the Bank of England, ECB, Bank of Japan and Swiss National Bank.

Central banks did everything in their power to sever the link between over-indebtedness and deflation. The United States monetary policy from August 2007 to March 2009 was characterised by a lengthening of loan maturities, broader collateral eligibility and the possibility for new players in the financial industry to refinance with the Federal Reserve. The ECB also changed the maturity structure of its refinancing operations, favouring three- and six-month operations over one-week operations.

As the original problem was uncertainty over the market valuation of financial assets, central banks were obliged to take on assets (that were not necessarily of excellent quality) on their books at prices different from the market price in order to avoid a banking liquidity crisis. The subprime crisis *ipso facto* transformed the role of central banks from a lender of last resort to an asset buyer/holder of last resort. Would Irving Fisher have wanted central banks to go to such lengths to avoid deflation?

Chapter 8

Exogenous Crises: Pandemics and Wars

Pandemics

The COVID-19 crisis, which is exogenous in nature, will have long-term consequences that will not disappear even as it ceases to be a health emergency and vaccination becomes widespread. On the face of it, China has emerged stronger from this crisis because it pulled out all the stops to deal with the health crisis it triggered, much as the United States did in response to the 1929 and 2008 financial crises. At the same time, China's communication has been steeped in lies and untruths, evidence of a frailty that is difficult to measure. The human and economic toll of the COVID-19 crisis is on the scale of a world war. The management of the health crisis involved bringing economic and social activity to an artificial standstill, which disrupted global value chains and transformed it into a full-blown crisis. Western states took on massive amounts of debt to finance an economy that was barely ticking over. Yet, no reparation will be paid by China. Furthermore, with the constitution of the World Health Organization (WHO) differing markedly from that of the International Atomic Energy Agency (IAEA), it does not have the investigative powers to determine *in situ* the origins of COVID-19 as it sees fit. So, finding a definitive cure without knowing and understanding the origin of this virus is mission impossible. Changing the WHO's constitution is not even on the agenda. Health remains a matter of national sovereignty. Yet, like the Chernobyl cloud, viruses do not stop at borders. As for the WHO, may we say that it should have the same prerogatives as the IAEA, whose own powers should be strengthened, as demonstrated by Russia's war on Ukraine.

The current pandemic has also raised awareness among the world's population that climate disruption could give rise to crises whose management could resemble that of the health crisis, with the issue once again being means and resources. For example, if climate change makes summers excessively hot, it is likely that we will once again be forced to stay indoors to protect ourselves from extreme temperatures.

We can ask ourselves whether, in the wake of the COVID-19 crisis, the European Union will "die by instalments" or whether, as a result of this economic upheaval, it will have to rethink the economic paradigm inherited from the Industrial Revolution and invent a new sustainable economic model in symbiosis with its environment. Will the growth generated by a genuine ecological turnaround be able to wipe out the debts accumulated since the oil crisis of the 1970s?

Unlike the crises of 1929 and 2008, the COVID-19 crisis was due to an exogenous shock caused by a new, highly contagious and virulent virus that spread across the planet and has undergone several mutations, severely disrupting economic activity. An external epidemiological shock went on to become an economic, social and psychological shock.

This was not Europe's first pandemic. In fact, it has experienced many over the centuries, which have often repeated until a cure was discovered. Compared with past outbreaks of bubonic plague or cholera, this pandemic stands out on account of the approach and management adopted by European governments in the 21st century. To keep the death toll down, many countries, including France, placed large swathes of the population in lockdown from the very start of the pandemic. In France, the first lockdown was ordered on 17 March and lasted until 11 May 2020.

During previous pandemics, lockdowns were limited to specific areas or towns. It was the first time in its history that all of France was placed on lockdown to check the spread of a disease. Can this be described as progress? Is this what the modern management of a pandemic looks like? What was not done in the Middle Ages was done in the 21st century. Admittedly, public health took precedence over the economy, but if the French health system had been more efficient and if the Institut Pasteur had had greater financial resources to develop a vaccine, France might not have been locked down, at any rate not for so long.

The entire economy ended up barely ticking over because of the lack of labour (with everyone being confined to their homes) and restricted access to the workplace from the very start of the pandemic. There was a supply-side shock as workers were in lockdown, considered as contact cases or ill. Social distancing and capacity restrictions in public places amplified the shock. Fear of catching the virus reduced productivity by modifying the frequency and nature of interactions. In addition, the virus mutated, becoming more contagious. The Omicron variant was far more contagious than the Delta variant, and while vaccination had slowed the transmission of the Wuhan and Delta variants, it proved less effective in the case of the Omicron variant.

By its very nature, the pandemic triggered a supply shock at the global level too. Value chains were disrupted at the start of the epidemic. People's movements were halted or severely impeded for periods at a time, creating a shockwave on the supply side, for example, in the agricultural sector, in which fruit and vegetable pickers are often foreign workers. The aviation sector was also hugely affected.

Two years after the start of the pandemic, while digitalisation, automation and productivity gains produced a positive supply shock, increases in the price of raw materials and transport and the fall in the labour participation rate[1] produced a negative supply shock. If, at the end of the crisis, the negative shock were to outweigh the positive one, growth would slow and inflation would rise.

During pandemics, demand can decline because, in a context of uncertainty, households set aside precautionary savings and businesses stop investing. Savings during the COVID-19 pandemic were forced rather than precautionary, as households were only able to buy "essentials" in-store during lockdowns. Paradoxically, during the first lockdown, shops selling only alcohol, which could in any case be bought in supermarkets, were allowed to stay open, whereas bookstores were ordered to close!

Strategic sectors, or those particularly affected by the pandemic, as well as all businesses, whether profitable or not before the crisis, were supported by state-guaranteed loans. As a result, two years after the start of the pandemic, the profit margin has increased spectacularly. The number of business failures in 2020 and 2021 has been lower than during the

---

[1]The labour force participation rate is calculated as the labour force divided by the total working-age population. The working-age population refers to people aged 15–64. https://data.oecd.org/emp/labour-force-participation-rate.htm.

2008 financial crisis, thanks to massive transfers of public funds to businesses.

This improvement in profitability in a time of crisis is all the more surprising given the rise in the prices of raw materials, energy and transport. In the euro area and the United States, investment picked up very quickly after the pandemic shock. By contrast, there has been a vertiginous fall in investment in the United Kingdom, where the effects of Brexit have been compounded by the effects of the pandemic.

Demand may also decline as a result of a fall in world trade. And indeed, there was a real but very brief fall, which was followed by a spectacular rebound.

The economy's forced-march digitalisation during the pandemic, spurred in particular by teleworking and the development of online commerce even for small and medium-sized businesses, made a major contribution to growth. Looking at these parameters, the conclusion is that France's growth would have been significant if another exogenous shock, Russia's war on Ukraine, had not followed close on the heels of the health crisis.

In previous pandemics, the death toll reshuffled the economic deck, as this led to labour shortages in the countries affected. Wages rose as a result, while the reduction in the working population led to a fall in economic activity. There was a direct correlation between the number of pandemic-related deaths, the fall in GDP and the redistribution of purchasing power. During the COVID-19 crisis, GDP fell dramatically, even before the rise in pandemic-related deaths. According to the IMF, economic activity contracted by 3.5% in the United States and by 6.6% in the euro area due to prolonged lockdowns. It contracted by 9.9% in the United Kingdom, as the effects of the pandemic were compounded by the effects of Brexit. At the global level, there was a 3.3% contraction in activity. Nor does there appear to be a strong correlation between the number of deaths and the contraction in economic activity, even though the number of deaths reached 158,370 in France[2] and 6.72 million worldwide[3] on 26 December 2022, assuming that countries such as China and Russia have indeed reported all cases.

It would seem that GDP tends rather to be inversely correlated to the virus's effective reproduction number (R_e). This measures the

---

[2] https://covid19.who.int/region/euro/country/fr.
[3] https://covid19.who.int/.

transmissibility of the COVID-19 virus, i.e. the average number of people in a population who can be contaminated by an infected individual at any specific time. When R_e decreases, a rebound in activity follows, as happened in the summer of 2020. Russia's war on Ukraine proved to be the exogenous shock that replaced the pandemic, which has not yet run its full course. For economic players, there is now a more pressing issue. The Great Influenza[4] pandemic followed in the wake of the First World War, whereas this time the COVID-19 pandemic came first.

The pandemic had a direct impact on the economy, disrupting the economic cycle. While the initial shock was identical for all European countries, the repercussions differed according to the weaknesses and dependencies of each country. The pandemic had a negative impact on certain sectors, such as tourism, on which countries such as France, Italy, Greece and Spain are heavily dependent. While the French were very proud of their healthcare system and had confidence in it, this external shock revealed the difficulties and shortcomings of a system that had, in fact, been bled dry. It also revealed the poor state of health of an ageing population. The French were shocked to discover that, just as the emperor in Hans Christian Andersen's tale, *The Emperor's New Suit*, the healthcare system "has nothing on at all".

The question is whether the inflation that built up during the COVID-19 crisis was monetary inflation (due to money creation to support the economy during the pandemic, involving the monetisation of public deficits) or cost-push inflation. The forced savings accumulated by households are not being spent. Therefore, this is not what has driven inflation. During the pandemic, demand decreased for services, whereas it increased for goods. This increase was driven by teleworking (with the equipping of employees working from home), online commerce, home relocations (with spending on redecoration and household equipment), thermal building renovation, business automation and renewable energy production. The upturn in manufacturing activity led to bottlenecks for semiconductors, raw materials and transport, which drove up prices for these goods and related services. It may therefore be that inflation came from the real economy.

Trust is an important factor in managing and then exiting a crisis. In France, the birthplace of microbiology pioneer Louis Pasteur, who invented vaccines against rabies and anthrax, trust in scientists and

---

[4]Also known by the common misnomer of "the Spanish flu".

consequently in vaccines waned over the course of the pandemic. The fact that these vaccines were developed abroad may have played a hand in all this. The high vaccination rate was only achieved because of the restrictions imposed by the French government, with the introduction of the health pass to begin with and then later the vaccination pass.

In its assessment of 2020 and 2021, the OECD explained when it published its *December 2021 Economic Outlook* that the economic recovery was dependent on the rapid rollout of effective vaccines:

> "The global recovery is continuing but its momentum has eased and is becoming increasingly imbalanced according to the OECD's latest Economic Outlook. The failure to ensure rapid and effective vaccination everywhere is proving costly with uncertainty remaining high due to the continued emergence of new variants of the virus. Output in most OECD countries has now surpassed where it was in late-2019 and is gradually returning to the path expected before the pandemic. However, lower-income economies, particularly ones where vaccination rates against COVID-19 are still low, are at risk of being left behind. [...] The recovery is also uneven within advanced economies. Employment is still relatively weak in the United States, but is already higher than its pre-pandemic level in the Euro Area. At the same time, United States GDP has recovered faster than Europe's. Different protection models mean different challenges looking ahead".

For the United States, the challenge was to get more people back into work; for Europe, it was to generate more growth.

This became even more of a challenge for Europe in February 2022, when Russia invaded Ukraine.

Wars

Large-scale armed conflicts are another type of exogenous crisis. The two world wars were the biggest external shocks ever experienced by humanity and the global economy. The loss of human life was colossal. Some 19 million people were killed in the First World War, of whom 9 million were civilians. The death toll reached 1.7 million in France and 2.5 million in Germany. Some 64 million people were killed as a result of the Second World War, of whom 42 million were civilians. Some 30 million

Europeans were displaced[5] because of the redrawing of borders, especially in Eastern Europe. Most of Europe's Jewish population perished, falling from 7 million before the war to just 1 million after. Some countries paid a higher toll than others: in Poland, the death toll reached 5,820,000, or 15% of its population, whereas in France, it reached 541,000, of which 330,000 were civilians.

A war is a shock not only for the workforce but also for another factor of production, as machinery, tools and buildings may be totally destroyed. A country's infrastructure, such as bridges, will also be at least partially destroyed. For economic activity to resume, countries may have to invest several times their pre-war GDP. In the case of France, after the First World War, this investment effort amounted to four times its 1913 GDP. These investments, made on credit, were added to the victors' war debts as well as to the war debts of the vanquished, besides which the latter also took on debts to pay the war reparations imposed by the victors. With hindsight, it is clear that after the Treaty of Versailles, the Central Powers could not cope with the weight of all these accumulated debts, often denominated in dollars, and that the only way out was therefore another war.

"Between 1913 and 1918, the public debt of the belligerents rose from 30 billion francs to 300 billion francs in France, from 18 billion to 197 billion in Britain, and from 6 billion to 168 billion in Germany, before taking into account the reparations provided for in the Treaty of Versailles. Amounts were borrowed by governments mainly from their central banks, which had the effect of converting public debt into means of payment. [...] The result was widespread inflation".[6]

Inflation soared on high in Germany. This, combined with the 1929 crisis, ultimately set the scene for a new exogenous crisis, the Second World War.

"The First World War [...] knocked the bottom out of the countries that were to become the G7, just as the 19th century had done to China and India. Monetary, budgetary and production frameworks came apart. As

---

[5]Centre Robert Schuman, Repères, Bilan de la Seconde Guerre Mondiale (en chiffres). http://www.centre-robert-schuman.org.
[6]Daniel, Jean-Marc (2021), p. 241.

soon as war was declared in August 1914, leading industrialised countries suspended the gold convertibility of their currencies. They
thought this would be a temporary measure. But in January 1915,
Britain, still the leading monetary and financial power, permanently
abandoned the Gold Standard and introduced exchange controls. The
principle of free movement of capital and fixed exchange rates established in 1844 was no more, so come 1918 a monetary system had to
be rebuilt".[7]

In his autobiography, *Die Welt von Gestern. Erinnerungen eines
Europäers*, Stefan Zweig [1881–1942] reminisced about his travels before
the First World War, writing that "no one had asked me about my national-
ity, my religion, my origin, and — fantastic as it may seem to the world
of today with its fingerprinting, visas, and police certificates — I had
travelled without a passport".[8] The rise of the bureaucratic and fiscal state,
as we know it today, had not insinuated itself into the everyday lives of
Europeans. Each world war has strengthened the state, and the COVID-19
pandemic has given it enormous power as never before over a digital
world in which every individual is entirely traceable and liable to control.
These exogenous crises have been external shocks that have shaken the
entire state architecture as well as the balance of power between individuals and the state, as well as between states.

> "The warring State of 1914 had not disappeared completely by 1919; it
> would go on to become the spendthrift State of the 20th century [...]
> justifying itself by claiming to be a welfare State. [...] In France,
> between 1817 and 1913, GDP grew by almost 50%, but public spending
> increased by only 20%. In 1913, it represented 13% of GDP. A century
> later, it had risen to 55%".[9]

A similar fate befell other European countries. The state's presence
in people's daily lives comes at an ever-increasing cost to public
finances and freedom, which is unlikely to be any less in the wake of the
COVID-19 pandemic.

---

[7] *Ibid.*, pp. 240–241.
[8] Zweig, Stefan (1943).
[9] Daniel, Jean-Marc (2021), p. 242.

The United States was originally a very inward-looking country with no interest in international affairs. However, having been called to the rescue by the Europeans to fight two wars that did not concern them, the United States came to the realisation that there were huge strategic and economic advantages to meddling in the affairs of other countries, and they have remained ever since what they puritanically call "the world's policeman". This role is now coveted by China. Russia's war on Ukraine could have been an opportunity to do just that. When Western powers are paying over the odds for oil and gas, access to a cheaper supply in fact matters more to China than wielding soft power. What's more, this conflict will weaken Russians, Ukrainians and Westerners alike. China will become the world leader that much quicker, as Europe and the United States will emerge weaker.

But what was the impact of the two world wars, two exogenous crises that were initially European, on the United States?

The outbreak of the Second World War in Europe triggered an exogenous shock that led to a period of inflation in the United States, much like the ones caused by the American Civil War and the First World War. What was different was that inflation was lower but lasted longer — for nine years, from September 1939 to August 1948. According to annual data, over this period, wholesale prices rose at an average rate of 8.2% per year; the implicit price deflator,[10] 6.5% per year; the stock of money, 12.3% per year (or slightly less than during the First World War, from 1914 to 1920, and by half as much as during the American Civil War, from 1861 to 1865); money income,[11] 10.7% per year; real income,[12] 4.2% per year; and velocity,[13] 1.7% per year.[14]

---

[10]Price deflator refers to the implicit deflators that are calculated by dividing an aggregate measured at current prices by the same aggregate measured at constant prices. See, INSEE, https://www.insee.fr/en/metadonnees/definition/c1715.

[11]Money income or nominal income refers to the actual flow of earnings measured in monetary units, not taking into account inflation, purchasing power or other factors that may affect the actual value of money income.

[12]Real income refers to the flow of earnings corresponding to the real purchasing power.

[13]Velocity of money (often reduced to velocity) refers to the average number of times in a given period (typically a year) that a unit of money is spent on buying the total amount of goods and services produced in the economy.

[14]Friedman, Milton (1952).

As with the First World War, prices surged when the war broke out, remained high for a year and then continued to rise. Surprisingly, prices rose less quickly once the United States became actively involved in the war.

Abiding by longstanding diplomatic practice, the United States maintained strict neutrality from September 1939 to November 1941. Neutrality was clearly demarcated diplomatically, but economically it was not, especially after France's fall. Britain ordered war supplies from the United States, which delivered them by ship and received payment in gold. Gold to the value of $2 billion was sent in exchange for war supplies before the Lend-Lease programme, which had the corollary of increasing the stock of money. The same phenomenon occurred at the start of the First World War. The difference compared with that period was that the Federal Reserve held $2 billion of government securities, which could have been sold at will to offset the effect of gold inflows, but were not. Between August 1939 and November 1941, wholesale prices rose by 23%.

Lend-Lease was an armament programme implemented by the United States to "sell, transfer title to, exchange, lend, lease, or otherwise dispose of [...] any defense article"[15] to allied nations. Under this programme, some $50 billion was spent by the United States by the end of the war.[16] Concurrently, the United States embarked on a rearming of the nation's ground and air forces. These defence programmes contributed to a rapid increase in industrial output, employment and wages.

Milton Friedman and Anna Schwartz termed the period from December 1941 to January 1946 the "period of wartime deficits",[17] as first the expanded defence programme and then the Lend-Lease programme led to a substantial increase in government expenditures. The authors explain that there was a more complete conversion to a "total war economy".[18] Pearl Harbor brought about a sharp increase in government expenditures, which nearly tripled from calendar 1941 to calendar 1942, before rising a further 50% from 1942 to 1943 and

---

[15]Lend-Lease, formally the Lend-Lease Act, introduced as "An Act to Promote the Defense of the United States" (Pub. L. 77–11, H.R. 1776, 55 Stat. 31, enacted 11 March 1941).

[16]Friedman, Milton and Schwartz, Anna Jacobson (1963), p. 550.

[17]*Ibid.*, p. 556.

[18]*Ibid.*, p. 557.

culminating at nearly $95 billion in 1944. From November 1941 to January 1946, the government debt outside the US government and the Federal Reserve System increased by $178 billion, of which some $69 billion was acquired by commercial banks.

Despite the Marshall Plan, a vast quantity of gold flowed into the United States from war-devastated countries wanting to purchase goods no longer available locally. From August 1945 to July 1946, the stock of money increased by $1.9 billion. It then increased by $1.1 billion from May 1947 to August 1948. Yet, the Federal Reserve behaved as if on the cusp of deflation, not raising interest rates to slow inflation.

As shown in this chapter, exogenous crises, such as pandemics or wars, have a strong and lasting impact on the economy. Unlike financial crises, no regulation can prevent these crises, for they originate outside the economic system.

The looming climate crisis is of a similar nature and will probably be on a much larger scale than a pandemic or world war.

Conclusion

It has to be conceded that Her Gracious Majesty Queen Elizabeth II did not obtain a satisfactory answer to her question as to why the crisis of 2008 occurred, nor was a totally convincing formulation employed, at least. Perhaps the answer should be stated in the form of a question: why talk about a crisis at all? Or, has the world ever known situations that were not crises?

For, with all the respect due to the monarch, it would be our contention that this matter should not be posed in the terms used by Her Majesty. What geologist can lay claim to having accurately predicted every earthquake? And yet, no one feels entitled or obligated to doubt the competence of geologists.

This issue was raised by French economist Jean Tirole, the recipient of the 2014 Nobel Prize in Economics, in his acceptance speech:

> "The great economist John Maynard Keynes once wrote: 'If economists could manage to get themselves thought of as humble, competent people on a level with dentists, that would be splendid.' 83 years and much research later, we would perhaps aspire to be compared with 'meteorologists' or 'doctors', whose scientific accomplishments have been truly outstanding and yet have to face challenges that are rather down-to-earth. Our failure to foresee or prevent the financial crisis is a sore reminder of the dangers of hubris. True enough, we had worked on most of its ingredients. But like a virus that keeps mutating, new dangers emerged when we thought we had understood and avoided the existing

ones. The need to be humble applies also to the field that was rewarded by the Prize".[1]

Humility is a laudable virtue, but lest economists forget, they are expected to provide practical answers to the problems facing society, particularly in terms of economic growth and well-being.

In the case of recurring crises, Pierre-Alain Muet's diagnosis of the 1993 crisis does provide some explanations. His view was that every crisis is the result of three mechanisms: the cycle as modelled by the Hansen–Samuelson oscillator, in which investment plays a major role; more or less speculative mechanisms associated with uncontrolled credit expansion; and misguided economic policies.

Over the longer run, what past experience shows is that, first, in order to respond to the issues it deals with, economic thought (political economy, later economics) looked at the situation of the dominant economy and expressed itself in the language of that economy. Thus, economics in the early 18th century sought to address the problems of the French economy and was written in French. In the 19th and early 20th centuries, when Britain was the dominant economy, economics expressed itself in English. Since 1950, the United States has taken over this role, and so English has remained the language of economics. Second, the economic sciences must be in a permanent state of questioning, ready for when the economy seizes up and a new crisis erupts.

Successive economic theories were developed, each supposed to provide better answers than their predecessors to changing problems. It can be considered that four economic schools have succeeded one another. At the end of the 18th century, the Physiocratic school, inspired by French economist and physician François Quesnay, held that economic growth driven by agriculture was the only viable response to the mounting public debt, which was then the overarching problem.

At the beginning of the 19th century, the classical school, which referred to Adam Smith but whose leader was David Ricardo, noted the limits of agriculture due to its diminishing returns. They also pointed to the political failure of physiocracy, reflected in the collapse of France, with its descent into "murderous war" in 1793 during the Reign of Terror. The classical school saw salvation in free trade and the worldwide spread

---

[1] Tirole, Jean (2014).

of "gentle commerce".[2] With fortune beginning to smile on Britain, it started to assert its intellectual dominance.

At the end of the 19th century, the growing efficiency of the productive system shook the classical citadel and gave rise to the neo-classical school of William S. Jevons, Alfred Marshall and Léon Walras. For these economists, it was about the equilibrium between an increasingly abundant supply and a demand nearing saturation. They saw the answer in unbridled competition.

By the middle of the 20th century, with the 1929 crisis having brought misery and sorrow in its wake, the stage was set for Keynesianism. Named after John Maynard Keynes, Keynesianism theorised what became known as the underemployment equilibrium, which it sees as sowing the seeds of political unrest. It explored the neutrality of money and the role of investment. It also theorised the business cycle, contending that crises were not fatalities and did not portend the inevitable advent of a totalitarian planning system advancing under the guise of socialism. Its answer was to plaster over the cracks in the economic edifice with bucketfuls of public investment financed by debt. John Maynard Keynes may have been British, but the school of thought he inspired accompanied the emergence of a new dominant economy, the United States. As a result, the centre of gravity in academia shifted to Boston and Chicago, with the likes of Alvin Hansen, Paul Samuelson and James Tobin.

Keynesianism still dominates the economic sciences, but in an amended form known as neo-Keynesianism. However, a new round of debates has opened, with the challenge being to formulate an improved body of theory addressing the problems posed by the 2008–2009 recession and, incidentally, the ironic remarks of Her Majesty, the Queen of England.

The fairly conventional, mainstream approaches to economics — a mix of contrived praises for central banks and the denunciation of finance, calls for public investment and concerns about the unprecedented levels of public debt — are under assault by two groups of economists seeking to develop a new body of operational theory.

---

[2]In his *Spirits of Laws*, French philosopher Charles de Secondat, Baron de Montesquieu, explained that commerce "polishes and refines the most barbarous", that "it is almost a general rule that wherever we find agreeable manners, there commerce flourishes; and that wherever there is commerce, there we meet with agreeable manners".

First, there are the New Classicals, such as Robert Lucas and Robert Barro, who see themselves as heirs to Ricardo and reformers of Milton Friedman's monetarism. They gave rise to RBCS and have no hesitation in denouncing the failure of Keynesianism, whether of old or in its modern version. Robert Lucas, during his acceptance speech for the 1995 Nobel Prize for Economic Sciences, stated that "Keynes's actual influence as a technical economist is pretty close to zero".

Their view is that the best response to any form of crisis is to dust down the ideas that guided the first economists, which were to ask the state not to get involved in trying to solve the problems labelled crisis, a term used incessantly. Robert Lucas delights in quoting a text from Jean-Baptiste Say's *A Treatise on Political Economy*: "It is next to impossible for a government, not only to do any good to national production by its interference, but even to avoid doing mischief".[3] The expression "national production" should be understood in its meaning at the start of the 20th century, therefore synonymous with the country's economy.

Referring to the legacy of that giant of economic science, David Ricardo, the New Classical School of Economics came as a timely reminder that all economic policy should ultimately be based on private competition and public parsimony.

Pitted against the New Classical School inspired by the writings of David Ricardo, the most imaginative heirs to Keynesianism are now the proponents of what became known as the Modern Monetary Theory (MMT).

The resurgence of inflation in the 20th century, which was the consequence of Keynesian policies and the attendant explosion in public debt, having contributed to these policies being called into question, the proponents of MMT made the inflation rate the yardstick for assessing economic policy. It is the inflation rate that determines the point at which the state must start to police itself and the central bank must stop buying back public debt securities.

For these economists, until inflation rears its head, the state can and must continue to take on debt financed by the creation of money by the central bank. They call for a systematic increase in public spending financed by central bank debt, with the goal being to support growth and maintain full employment. As for taxation, its primary purpose is not to fund government spending but to meet the state's natural objectives as

---

[3] Say, Jean-Baptiste (1803).

identified by the economist Richard Musgrave in his 1959 book,[4] namely the implementation of an income redistribution policy to correct inequalities and a policy to combat externalities, aimed notably at reducing carbon consumption. The increase in public spending would therefore only reach its ceiling at the point where inflation manifests itself. And at the global level, besides cyclical tensions, inflation will not be on the agenda until the rural exodus in India and Africa has been completed and not for as long as there is still a huge pool of underemployed labour.

The monetary and, therefore, economic dynamics of the world, according to MMT, no longer rely on the gold digger's pickaxe or on the more or less measured enthusiasm of the banker but on the expansion of public demand.

Tomorrow's world is going to have to decide whether, in order to limit crises, it should put its trust in free entrepreneurs spurred on by competition or allow itself to be guided by the technocrats guaranteeing outlets for entrepreneurs and jobs for everyone, thanks to an unrestrained ability to create money.

And what if we could ask Her Majesty Queen Elizabeth II for her opinion?

---

[4]Musgrave, Richard (1959).

Bibliography

Aftalion, Albert (1913). *Les crises périodiques de surproduction*. Paris: Librairie des sciences politiques et sociales.

Allais, Maurice (1993). *Les conditions monétaires d'une économie de marchés: des enseignements du passé aux réformes de demain* (The Monetary Conditions of an Economy of Markets: from the Teaching of the Past to the Reforms of Tomorrow), Revue d'économie politique, Vol. 103, No. 3 (May–June 1993).

Barber, William J. (1985). *New Era to New Deal: Herbert Hoover, the Economists, and American Economic Policy 1921–1933*. Cambridge University Press.

Bernanke Ben S. and Blinder, Alan S. (1988). Credit, money and aggregate demand. *American Economic Review Papers and Proceedings*, 78(2), 435–439.

Bilan de la Seconde Guerre mondiale (en chiffre), site internet du centre Robert Schuman, uploaded in 2011: http://www.centre-robertschuman.org/userfiles/files/REPERES%20-%20module%201-2-0%20-%20notice%20-%20Bilan%20de%20la%20Seconde%20Guerre%20mondiale%20-%20FR%20-%20final.pdf.

Boyer, Robert (1978). *Économie politique des capitalismes*. Paris: La Découverte.

Boyer, Robert and Mistral, Jacques (1978). *Accumulation, Inflation, Crises*. Paris: Puf.

Boyer, Robert (1986). *La théorie de la régulation: une analyse critique*. Paris: La Découverte.

Boyer, Robert (2022). *Political Economy of Capitalisms*. Paris: La Découverte, p. 2.

Céline, Louis-Ferdinand (1933). *Voyage au bout de la nuit*. Paris: Denoël et Steele.

Céline, Louis-Ferdinand (1936). *Mort à crédit*. Paris: Denoël.

Comment fonctionne l'assouplissement quantitatif? site internet de la Banque centrale européenne, uploaded 9 December 2016: https://www.ecb.europa.eu/ecb/educational/explainers/show-me/html/app_infographic.fr.html.

Coquelin, Charles (1854). *Dictionnaire de l'économie politique*. Paris: Guillaumin et Cie.

Daniel, Jean-Marc (2021). *Histoire de l'économie mondiale. Des chasseurs-cueilleurs aux cybertravailleurs*. Paris: Tallandier, pp. 301–302.

Daniel, Jean-Marc (2021). *Il était une fois l'argent magique*. Paris: Le Cherche midi.

Daniel, Jean-Marc (2022). *La Politique économique*. Paris: Que sais-je?

Engels, Friedrich and Marx, Karl (2017). *Manifeste du parti communiste (1848)*. Paris: Librio.

Fisher, Irving (1906). *The Nature of Capital and Income*. New York: Macmillan.

Fisher, Irving (1907). *The Rate of Interest. Its Nature, Determination and Relation to Economic Phenomena*. New York: Macmillan.

Fisher, Irving (1911). *The Purchasing Power of Money. Its Determination and Relation to Credit, Interest and Crises*. New York: Macmillan.

Fisher, Irving (1930). *The Theory of Interest*. New York: Macmillan.

Fisher, Irving (1932). *Booms and Depressions: Some First Principles*. New York: Adelphi Company.

Friedman, Milton (1952). Price, income, and monetary changes in three wartime periods. *The American Economic Review*, 42(2), 612–625. http://www.jstor.org/stable/1910632.

Friedman, Milton and Schwartz, Anna Jacobson (1963). *A Monetary History of the United States, 1867–1960*. National Bureau of Economic Research Publications, Princeton University Press, Chapter 7.

Gagnon, Joseph, Raskin, Matthew, Remache, Julie and Sack, Brian (2010). *Large-Scale Asset Purchases by the Federal Reserve: Did They Work?* Federal Reserve Bank of New York Staff Reports, no. 441. https://www.newyorkfed.org/medialibrary/media/research/staff_reports/sr441.pdf.

Galbraith, John K. (1955). *The Great Crash 1929*. Boston: Houghton Mifflin.

Gaz de schiste aux États-Unis: enjeux stratégiques et politiques, site internet de l'École de guerre économique, uploaded 10 February 2022: https://www.ege.fr/infoguerre/gaz-de-schiste-aux-etats-unis-enjeux-strategiques-et-politiques.

Gide, Charles (1884). *Principes d'économie politique*. Paris: L. Larose. https://www.newyorkfed.org/medialibrary/media/research/staff_reports/sr441.pdf.

International Monetary Fund (2010). *Annual Report 2010 Supporting a Balanced Global Recovery*, p. 9.

Ionesco, Eugène (1963). *Exit the King*. New York: Grove Press.

Juglar, Clément (1862). *Des crises commerciales et leur retour périodique en France, en Angleterre et aux États-Unis*. Paris: Guillaumin et Cie.

Kafka, Franz, A little fable. East of the Web. http://www.eastoftheweb.com/cgi-bin/version_printable.pl?story_id=LittFabl.shtml.

Keynes, John Maynard (1931). *Essays in Persuasion*. London: Macmillan.

Keynes, John Maynard (1936). *The General Theory of Employment, Interest, and Money*.

Keynes, John Maynard (1972). *Essays in Persuasion*, Vol. 9, The Collected Writings. New York: St Martin's Press, p. 311. The essay is entitled *Liberals and Labour*.

Kissinger, Henry (2020). *Years of Renewal*. Touchstone/Simon & Schuster.

Kondratieff, Nicolaï (1992). *Les Grands Cycles de la conjuncture (1926)*. Paris: Economica.

Krugman, Paul (2008). *The Return of Depression Economics and the Crisis of 2008*. New York: Norton & Company.

Krugman, Paul, Obstfeld, Maurice and Melitz, Marc (2009). *International Economics: Theory and Policy*, Boston: Pearson Addison-Wesley.

Leshem, Dotan (2016). Retrospectives: What did the ancient Greeks mean by oikonomia? *Journal of Economic Perspectives*, 30(1), 225–238.

Mankiw, Gregory N. and Taylor, Mark P. (2017). *Principles of Economics*. Boston: Cengage.

McCracken, Paul (1977). Towards full employment and price stability — A report to the OECD by a group of independent experts, Paris, OECD.

Minsky, Hyman P. (1986). *Stabilizing an Unstable Economy*. Yale University Press, Ex-library edition, Preface and Acknowledgments to the First Edition, p. X.

Mishkin, Frederic (1986). *The Economics of Money, Banking and Financial Markets*. Boston: Little, Brown & Company.

Mishkin, Frederic S. (2013). *Monnaie, banque et marchés financiers*. Paris: Pearson, 10e éd., p. 657.

Mitchell, Wesley C. (1913). *Business Cycles*. Berkeley: University of California Press.

Muet, Pierre-Alain (1994). *La récession de 1993 réexaminée*, Revue de l'OFCE, no. 49, pp. 103–123.

Musgrave, Richard (1959). *The Theory of Public Finance*. New York: McGraw-Hill.

Organisation for Economic Co-Operation and Development (1977). OECD economic outlook No. 22, Edition 1977/2. https://www.oecd-ilibrary.org/

economics/data/oecd-economic-outlook-statistics-and-projections/
oecd-economic-outlook-no-22_data-00144-en.

OECD (2006). *OECD Employment Outlook, Boosting Jobs and Incomes*. https://
www.oecd.org/els/emp/38569368.pdf.

OECD (2009). OECD strategic response to the financial and economic crisis —
Contributions to the global effort. https://www.oecd.org/economy/42061463.
pdf.

OECD (2011). *OECD at 50: Evolving Paradigms*. https://www.oecd.org/
economy/outlook/48010330.pdf.

Orieux, Jean (1999). *Voltaire*. Paris: Flammarion.

Reagan, Ronald (1982). *Message to the Congress Transmitting the Annual
Economic Report of the President*. https://www.reaganlibrary.gov/archives/
speech/message-congress-transmitting-annual-economic-report-president.

Ricardo, David (1816). *On the Principles of Political Economy, and Taxation*.
London: John Murray, Albemarle-Street, p. 330.

Rossi, Pellegrino (1840). *Cours d'économie politique*. Paris: Joubert.

Say, Jean-Baptiste (1803). *A Treatise on Political Economy*, 6th edn., based on
the 4th–5th editions, Book I, Chapter XVII, of the Effect of Government
Regulations Intended to Influence Production. https://www.econlib.org/
library/Say/sayT.html?chapter_num=19#book-reader.

Say, Léon and Chailley, Joseph (dir.). (1889–1892), *Nouveau dictionnaire
d'économie politique*. Paris: Guillaumin et Cie.

Schumpeter, Alois (1931). The present world depression: A tentative diagnosis.
American Economic Review. Supplement.

Sen, Ashish Kumar (2021). *German Reunification: 'It Was Nothing Short of a
Miracle'*, United States Institute for Peace, https://www.usip.org/
publications/2021/02/german-reunification-it-was-nothing-short-miracle.

Sismondi, Simonde de (1819). *Nouveaux principes d'économie politique*.

Talleyrand-Périgord, Charles-Maurice (de). (2002). *Talleyrand en verve: Mots,
propos, aphorismes*. Horay.

Tirole, Jean (2014). Nobel Prize acceptance speech, Nobel Prize Banquet. https://
www.tse-fr.eu/sites/default/files/medias/jean_tirole_acceptance_speech.pdf.

Vernimmen, Pierre (2022). *Finance d'entreprise*. Paris: Dalloz. https://www.
vernimmen.net/Pratiquer/Glossaire/definition/D%C3%A9flation.html.

Werner, Richard A. (2 September 1995). *Recovery through 'Quantitative
Monetary Easing'*. Nikkei, p. 26. https://eprints.soton.ac.uk/340476/1/
Translation_Werner_QE_ Nikkei_Sep_1995_final1.pdf.

WHO Coronavirus (COVID-19) Dashboard, https://covid19.who.int/region/euro/
country/fr.

WHO Coronavirus (COVID-19) Dashboard, https://covid19.who.int/.

Zweig, Stefan (1943). *The World of Yesterday: Memoirs of a European*.
New York: The Viking Press.

Index